The Art of Personality Development

(Steps to Success)

Namrata Palta

Lotus Press

4735/22, Prakash Deep Building,
Ansari Road, Darya Ganj,
New Delhi - 110002.

Lotus Press Publishers & Distributors
Unit No. 220, Second Floor, 4735/22, Prakash Deep Building,
Ansari Road, Darya Ganj, New Delhi-110002
Ph.: 41325510, 09811838000
E-mail: lotuspress1984@gmail.com
Visit us : www.lotuspress.co.in

The Art of Personality Development

ISBN: 978-81-8382-327-2

Published by: **Lotus Press Publishers & Distributors** New Delhi - 110002
Printed at: **Bharat Offset Works,** *Delhi*

The Art of Personality Development

(Steps to Success)

Published by
Lotus Press Publishers & Distributors

PREFACE

Hi Young readers!!

This book has been designed keeping in mind the drastic changes and immense requirement of communication for children. Considering that most schools now follow the CCE method where communication skills is mandatory for success and good grading, the book contains all the elements like pronunciation, confidence-building, presentation skills and vocabulary.

It is required that a child goes through all the six sections so as to develop a strong and impressive personality which would make him/her a winner in life.

So happy reading!!!

–Author

CONTENTS

Chapter 1-SPEECH/DEBATES/ PRESENTATION IN SCHOOL

Good presenters always use language (sometimes single words, sometimes phrases) which shows where they are in their presentation. These 'signposts' make it easier for the audience to:

- follow the structure of the presentation
- understand the speaker more easily
- get an idea of the length and content of the presentation.

The sentences and phrases below follow the logical progression of a well-balanced presentation.

Opening/Body/Closing Lines

Opening Lines

It is mandatory to start your speech with a good line. Whenever we start a speech we can introduce it with the following lines:

Hello everybody, My name is ________________and I will be presenting on the topic_______________.

Body of Speech

This has to be designed according to the time limit

Closing Lines

It is always a good idea to end with a slogan or proverbial use.

Welcoming:

- *Good morning Teachers and everyone present:*

Introducing yourself:

- *My name is Megha Singh and I am here to speak on the topic:*

Introducing your presentation:

- *The purpose of today's presentation is to … .*
- *The purpose of my presentation today is to … .*
- *In today's presentation I'd like to … show you … ./ explain to you how … .*
- *In today's presentation I'm hoping to … give you an update on… ./ give you an overview of… .*
- *In today's presentation I'm planning to … look at … ./ explain … .*

You can also outline your presentation to give the audience a clear overview of what they can expect:

- *In today's presentation I'm hoping to cover three points:*
- *firstly, … , after that we will look at … and finally I'll … .*
- *In today's presentation I'd like to cover three points:*
- *firstly, … , secondly … and finally … .*

Explaining that there will be time for questions at the end:

- *If you have any questions you'd like to ask, please leave them until the end, when I'll be happy to answer them.*
- *If there are any questions you'd like to ask, please leave them until the end, when I'll do my best to answer them.*

Starting the presentation:

- *To begin with … .*
- *To start with … .*

- *Let's start by looking at ... .*
- *Let's start by looking at ... .*
- *I'd like to start by looking at ... .*
- *Let's start with / start by looking at ... .*

Closing a section of the presentation:

- *So, that concludes* [title of the section]... .
- *So, that's an overview of ... .*
- *I think that just about covers ... .*

Beginning a new section of the presentation:

- *Now, let's move on to ... .*
- *Now, let's take a look at ... .*
- *Now I'd like to move on to ... .*
- *Next I'd like to take a look at ... .*
- *Moving on to the next part, I'd like to ... .*
- *Moving on to the next section, let's take a look at ... .*

Concluding and summarising the presentation:

- *Well, that brings us to the end of the final section. Now, I'd like to summarise by ... .*
- *That brings us to the end of the final section. Now, if I can just summarise the main points again.*
- *That concludes my presentation. Now, if I can just summarise the main points.*
- *That's an overview of ... . Now, just to summarise, let's quickly look at the main points again.*

Finishing and thanking:

- *That brings the presentation to an end.*
- *That brings us to the end of my presentation.*

Inviting questions:

- *If anyone has any questions, I'll be pleased to answer them.*
- *If anyone has any questions, I'll do my best to answer them.*

- *If anyone has any questions, please feel free to ask them now.*
- *If anyone has any questions, please feel free to ask them and I'll do my best to answer.*

Referring to a point previously made:

- *As I mentioned earlier ....*
- *As we saw earlier ....*
- *You may recall that we said ....*
- *You may recall that I explained ....*

Dealing with (difficult) questions:

- *I'll come back to that question later if I may.*
- *I'll / We'll come back to that question later in my presentation.*
- *I'll / We'll look at that point in more detail later on.*
- *Perhaps we can look at that point at the end / a little later.*

Other phrases and key presentation language:

[word, phrase]	[meaning, function]
Briefly	...'very quickly'
take a look at	...'look at'
take a brief look at	...'quickly look at'
return to	...'go back', 'explain again'
I'll outline	...'I will explain'
here we can see	...to draw attention to specific point on a slide
as you can see here	...to draw attention to a specific point on a slide
(let's) move on to	...to start a new subject
(let's) continue with	...to start a new subject
(let's) continue by looking at	...to start a new subject
to illustrate this point	...when giving an example

let's, we can, we will ...using 'we' and 'us' instead of 'I' connects you to your audienc

Body Language

YOUR BODY

Your body communicates different impressions to the audience. People not only listen to you, they also watch you. Slouching tells them you are indifferent or you do not care even though you might care a great deal!

On the other hand, displaying good posture tells your audience that you know what you are doing and you care deeply about it. Also, a good posture helps you to speak more clearly and effectively.

Eye Contact

- This helps to regulate the flow of communication.
- It signals interest in others and increases the speaker's credibility.
- Speakers who make eye contact, open the flow of communication and convey interest, concern, warmth and credibility.

Facial Expressions

Smiling is a powerful cue that transmits happiness, friendliness, warmth, and liking. So, if you smile frequently you will be perceived as more likable, friendly, warm and approachable.

Smiling is often contagious and others will react favourably.

Gestures

- If you fail to gesture while speaking, you may be perceived as boring and stiff.
- A lively speaking style captures attention, makes the material more interesting and facilitates understanding.

  Posture and body orientation: You communicate numerous messages by the way you talk and move.
- Standing erect and leaning forward communicates that you are approachable, receptive and friendly

Everyday Conversation

CONVERSATION PHRASES

- **Simple agreement**
  1. I agree.
  2. I really agree with you.
  3. I think you are right.
  4. I couldn't agree with you more.
  5. You said it.
  6. Can't say I don't agree.
  7. I'm with you on this.
  8. I partly agree.
  9. I agree on this but not that.
  10. It's partly true.

- **Track 2 - Accepting/Declining/Expressing acceptance**
  - I accept your point.

- Please accept this on our behalf.
- Sorry, I can't accept this.
- I'm 100% with you on this!
- Great idea.
- I'll take it.
- Sorry, I can't take it.
- Accept my apology.

- **Track 3 - Simple disagreement or refusal**
    - I disagree with you.
    - Everyone has own opinion, right?
    - I think you're wrong on this.
    - I'm sorry but I have to refuse your request.
    - You're wrong.
    - No way!
    - You've got to be kidding!
    - How can you even say that?
    - Where is your logic?

- **Track 4 - Strong disagreement**
    - I completely disagree with you.
    - You are very wrong to say that.
    - I totally disagree with you.
    - I can't find myself to agree with you.
    - You're dead wrong.
    - You're way wrong.
  - **Part 1 - Apologies**
    - o I'm sorry...
    - o I'm very sorry...

- I'm terribly sorry...
- Excuse me...
- Pardon me...
- I apologize...
- I'm afraid...

• **Part 2 - Explaining Oneself , Accepting Responsibility**

- ...I wasn't very well yesterday
- ...I didn't see you
- ...It won't happen again
- ...I'll be more careful next time
- ...I'll finish it before I go home
- ...It's my fault
- ...It's all my fault

• **Talking about your background**

- Originally I'm from....
- I was (born and) brought up in...
- I come from a sporty/musical family.
- My proudest moment was...-ing
- I've always dreamt of –ing/ wanted to... .

Describing your language ability

- I'm fluent in Polish.
- I speak Spanish reasonably well.
- I can get by in Portuguese.
- I speak French but it is a bit rusty.
- I know a few words of Japanese.
- I wish I could speak Italian.

like, such as and that sort of thing

- o I like music such as opera, choral music and classical music.
- o I really love modern music like house, rap, reggae, and hip hop.

After one or two examples, we can use an expression meaning 'et cetera'.

- o I'm fond of opera and that sort of thing.
- o I like jazz, rock and that sort of thing.

Showing a lot of interest

- Wow!
- Really?
- (That's) interesting!
- (That's) fantastic!

- **Simple good-byes (Formal)**
  - o Good-bye
  - o Stay in touch.
  - o It was nice meeting you.
  - o I hope to see you soon.

Simple good-byes (Informal)

- o Bye.
- o See you.
- o Talk to you later.
- o Catch up with you later.
- o Nice seeing you.

Leaving a place (Formal)

- o I have to leave here by noon.

- o Is it okay if we leave your home at 9 p.m.?
- o What do you say we leave work a little earlier today?
- o Would you mind if I leave the dinner before it ends?
- o I need to depart for the airport in one hour.

Leaving a place (Informal)

- o I got to go now.
- o I'll be leaving in 20 minutes.

General greetings (Formal)

1. Hello!
2. How are you?
3. How are you doing?
4. How is everything?
5. How's everything going?
6. How have you been keeping?
7. I trust that everything is well.

General greetings (Informal)

1. Hi.
2. What's up?
3. Good to see you.
4. How are things (with you)?
5. How's it going?
6. How's life been treating you?

Greeting a person you haven't seen for a long time (Formal)

1. It has been a long time.
2. It's been too long.
3. What have you been up to all these years?

4. It's always a pleasure to see you.
5. How long has it been?
6. I'm so happy to see you again.

Greeting a person you haven't seen for a long time (Informal)

- o How come I never see you?
- o It's been such a long time.
- o Long time no see.
- o Where have you been hiding?
- o It's been ages since we last met.

- **How to interrupt**
  - Actually...
  - Excuse me...
  - I'm sorry, but...
  - I just want to say...
  - May I interrupt here?
  - Do you mind if I say something?
- **Introducing paraphrasing**
  - So you mean....
  - What you mean is...
  - What you're saying is...
  - So what you mean to say is...
  - Let me get this clear...
  - Let me get this straight,...
    - o Could I use your phone?
    - o ...Might I possibly use your phone?
    - o ...Sorry to trouble you, but do you mind if I use your phone?

- o ...Would you mind if I used your phone?
- o ...May I use your phone?
- o ...Can I use your phone?
- o ...I wonder if I could use your phone.

- **How was...?**

How was your weekend?

It was lovely. How was yours?	(great)
It was terrible.	(really bad)
It was nice.	(fine)
A bit boring.	(not very interesting)

Link words: Then/after that

- o We had a drink. Then we went to the cinema.
- o OR we had a drink, and then we went to the cinema.
- o I went shopping. After that I met my sister.
- o OR I went shopping and after that, I met my sister.

Hesitation Strategies - Conversation Time Fillers

Often we want to give ourselves thinking time before we answer a question, especially if we don't understand it! Here are four techniques:

Techniques	*Examples*	*Advantages*	*Disadvantages*
Pretend you haven't heard	*Pardon?* *Sorry?* *Eh?*	Simple – only one word to remember.	Everyone does it.
Repeat the question?	*you mean... what is forty-five divided by nine?*	Lots of thinking time.	Can you the remember

Use delaying noises	*Well...* *Um...* *Er...*	You can use them several times in the same sentence.	If you use them too often you sound stupid.
Use *it depends*	*It depends. It depends on (the situation). Sorry? You want to know what I think about this? Well...um... it depends, really.*	You will sound intelligent. (Stroke your chin at the same time).	You can only use it when there is more than one possible answer.

- Don't forget that you can use more than one technique.

Given below is a comprehensive list of proverbs and quotations which can be used for good speeches:

Proverbs and Slogans to Use

Alphabetical List - A

(Page 1 : A bad excuse → a hungry wolf)

A bad excuse is better than none.	Always give an excuse, even if it's a poor one.
A bad penny always turns up.	An unwanted or disreputable person constantly comes back.
A bad tree does not yield good apples.	A bad parent does not raise good children.
A bad workman blames his tools.	Blaming the tools for bad workmanship is an excuse for lack of skill.
A barking dog seldom bites.	Someone who constantly makes threats rarely carries them out.

A bird in hand is worth two in a bush.
It is better to keep what you have rather than to risk losing it by searching for something better.

A black plum is as sweet as a white.
People should not be judged by their appearance.

A book holds a house of gold.
There is a wealth of knowledge in books.

A broken friendship may be soldered but will never be sound.
Friendships can be rebuilt after a dispute but will never be as strong as before.

A burden of one's own choice is not felt.
Something difficult seems easier when it is done voluntarily.

A burnt child dreads the fire.
A bad experience will make people stay away from certain things.

A burnt child dreads the fire.
A bad experience will make people stay away from certain things.

A calm sea does not make a skilled sailor.
A person shows their competence or ability when difficulties arise.

A cat has nine lives.
Cats can survive many accidents because they land on their feet without injury.

(Nine lives = 3 years to play, 3 years to stray, 3 years to stay.)

A chain is no stronger than its weakest link.
The strength of a group depends on each individual member.

A change is as good as a rest.
A change in routine is often as refreshing as a break or a holiday.

A constant guest is never welcome.	If you come to visit too often, your host will be less pleased to see you.
A danger foreseen is half avoided.	If you are prepared to face a problem or difficulty, it will be easier to deal with.
A day of sorrow is longer than a month of joy.	Time goes by very quickly when you are happy, and very slowly when you are sad.
A drop of ink may make a million think.	A thought expressed in writing (perhaps published in a newspaper) can influence a large number of people.
A dry March, a wet April and a cool May fill barn and cellar and bring much hay.	Harvest predictions are made according to the weather.
A fault confessed is half redressed.	Confession is the beginning of forgiveness.
A flower blooms more than once.	If you miss an occasion, you can avail yourself of it another time.
A fly will not get into a closed mouth. **A closed mouth catches no flies.**	If you learn when to keep silent you will avoid trouble.
A fool and his money are (soon) easily parted.	A foolish person usually spends money carelessly.
A fool at forty is a fool for ever.	If a person hasn't matured by the age of 40, he never will.

A friend in need is a friend indeed.	Someone who helps you when you are in trouble, is a real friend.
A friend to all is a friend to none.	Someone who is a friend to everyone makes none of them feel special.
A friend's eye is a good mirror.	A real friend will tell you the truth.
A good beginning makes a good end.	If a task is carefully planned, there's a better chance that it will be well done.
A good conscience is a soft pillow.	You sleep well when you have nothing to be guilty about.
A good example is the best sermon.	Giving a good example is better than giving advice.
A good name is better than a good face.	A good reputation is better than a good appearance.
A growing youth has a wolf in his belly.	Young boys eat a lot / are often hungry.
A guilty conscience needs no accuser.	If you know that you have done something wrong, you don't need anyone to tell you that you're guilty.
A handful of patience is worth more than a bushel of brains.	Patience is more precious than intelligence.
A happy heart is better than a full purse.	Happiness is better than wealth.
A heavy purse gives to a light heart.	When you have money you feel more cheerful and secure.

A hungry belly has no ears.
A hungry person is totally concentrated on their need for food and nothing else interests them.

A hungry wolf is fixed to no place.
A desperate person will go from place to place when they need to satisfy their needs.

Alphabetical List - A

(Page 2 : A lender nor borrower be   absence makes the heart grow fonder)

A lender nor borrower be.
Do not lend or borrow money.

A leopard cannot change its spots.
It is impossible for a bad or unpleasant person to become good or pleasant.

A lie begets a lie.
Telling one lie will lead you to tell another one.

A little fire is quickly trodden out.
If you deal with a minor problem quickly, it will not become a major issue.

A little of what you fancy does you good.
It's okay to give into a little temptation occasionally.

A loaded wagon makes no noise.
Really wealthy people do not talk about money.

A loveless life is living death.
Without affection, life is difficult.

A man can die but once.
If death comes now, you will not have to experience it later.

A man is as old as he feels himself to be.
Your age doesn't matter as long as you are fit and healthy.

A man is judged by his deeds, not by his words.	A person is judged on what he/she actually does, not on what they say they will do.
A man is known by the company he keeps.	A person's character is judged by the type of people with whom they spend their time.
A monkey in silk is a monkey no less.	No matter how someone dresses, it's the same person underneath.
A new broom sweeps clean	(but the old brush knows all the corners...) A newly-appointed person often makes changes quickly .
A nod is as good as a wink (to a blind horse/ man).	A hint or a subtle signal is enough to convey meaning to someone who is ready to understand.
A picture paints a thousand words.	A picture is better than a long description.
A problem shared is a problem halved. (Also: A worry shared is a worry halved.)	It is easier to deal with a problem when you discuss it with someone.
A rising tide lifts all boats.	Refers to something that will be helpful to all.
A rolling stone gathers no moss	If a person keeps moving from place-to-place, they gain neither friends nor possessions.Another interpretation is that, by moving often, one avoids being tied down!
A rotten apple spoils the barrel.	A dishonest or immoral person can have a bad influence on a group.

A smooth sea never made a skilled mariner.	Overcoming adversity leads to competence.
A soft answer turneth away wrath.	If your reply is polite and tactful you will avoid anger.
A stitch in time saves nine.	If you deal with a problem at an early stage you will save time and prevent it from getting worse.
A stumble may prevent a fall.	Correcting a small mistake may help you to avoid making a bigger one.
A swallow does not make the summer.	One good event does not mean that everything is alright.
A watched pot never boils.	If you wait anxiously for something to happen, it seems to take a long time.
A wise head keeps a still tongue.	An intelligent person knows when to stay silent.
A young idler, an old beggar.	If you don't work, you won't have any money when you're old.
Absence makes the heart grow fonder	When you are away from someone you love, you love them even more.

Alphabetical List - A

(Page 3 : Accidents will happen ask me no question)

Accidents will happen	Some unfortunate events must be accepted as inevitable.
Actions speak louder than words.	What a person actually does is more important than what they say they will do.

Adversity makes strange bed fellows.	People of all origins who share the same misfortune are drawn together.
Advice is cheap.	It doesn't cost anything to offer advice.
Advice is least heeded when most needed.	When a problem is serious, people often do not follow the advice given.
Advisors run no risks.	It's easier to give advice than to act.
After dinner rest a while, after supper walk a while.	Dinner is called 'lunch' nowadays and supper has become 'dinner'.
Agree, for the law is costly.	A compromise is better than an expensive lawsuit.
All cats are grey in the dark.	People are undistinguished until they have made a name for themselves.
All covet, all lose.	If you try to obtain everything, you risk losing everything.
All days are short to industry and long to idleness.	Time goes by slowly when you have nothing to do.
All good things come to those who wait.	If you are patient you will be rewarded.
All that glitters is not gold.	Appearances can be deceptive.
All in good time.	Be patient. Things will happen when the time is right.
All is fair in love and war.	Things that are done in love or war can often be excused.

All's well that ends well.	There is a solution to everything even if there are doubts.
All roads lead to Rome.	There are many different ways to reach an objective.
All things grow with time -except grief.	As time goes by, grief subsides little by little.
All things are difficult before they are easy.	With practice everything becomes easier.
All work and no play makes Jack a dull boy.	Everybody needs a certain amount of relaxation. It is not good to work all the time.
An apple a day keeps the doctor away.	Eating an apple every day can help to keep you healthy.Other interpretation: A small preventive treatment wards off serious problems.
An empty purse frigh-tens away friends.	When one's financial situation deteriorates, friends tend to disappear.
An Englishman's home is his castle.	An Englishman's home is a place where he feels safe, enjoys privacy and can do as he wishes.
An idle brain is the devil's workshop.	When you are busy working, you avoid temptation.
An old fox is not easily snared.	A person of experience is difficult to fool or manipulate.
An onion a day keeps everyone away.	A humoristic version of "an apple a day..."
An ounce of discretion is worth a pound of wit.	It is better to be cautious and discreet than to try to be funny.
An ounce of prevention	It is easier to prevent something

is worth a pound of cure.	from happening than to repair the damage or cure the disease later.
Anger is the one thing made better by delay.	When you are angry, it is best not to speak or act immediately.
Another day, another dollar.	A job may be hard or tedious but at least there is some financial reward.
Any time means no time.	If the date of an event remains vague, it will never happen.
April showers bring May flowers.	Something bad or unpleasant today may bring good things in the future.
As you sow, so shall you reap.	You have to accept the consequences of your actions.
Ask me no questions, I'll tell you no lies.	There are subjects one would rather not discuss.

Alphabetical List - B

(Bad news travels fast ... a burnt child dreads the fire)

Bad news travels fast.	People tend to circulate bad news very quickly (accidents, illness, etc.).
(A) bad tree does not yield good apples.	A bad parent does not raise good children.
(A) bad workman blames his tools.	Blaming tools for bad workmanship is an excuse for lack of skill.
Be just before you are generous.	Make sure all your debts are paid before you start offering help to others.
Beauty is only skin deep.	A person's character is more important than their appearance.

Beauty is in the eye of the beholder.	Different people have different tastes.
Beauty is the wisdom of women.Wisdom is the beauty of men.	No comment!
Be swift to hear, slow to speak.	Listen carefully before speaking.
(The) best helping hand is at the end of your sleeve.	The best way to get something done is to do it yourself.
Better an egg today than a hen tomorrow.	It is preferable to have something sure now than the possibility of something better later.
Better be alone than in bad company.	Be careful in the choice of the people you associate with.
Better be the head of a dog than the tail of a lion.	It's better to be the leader of a small group than a subordinate in a bigger one.
Better flatter a fool than fight him.	It's better to avoid disputes with stupid people.
Better to drink the milk than to eat the cow.	Be careful not to destroy the source of your income or welfare.
Better the devil you know than the devil you don't know.	It's better to deal with someone difficult but familiar than change and risk dealing with somebody worse.
Better late than never.	It's better to do something, even if it's late, than not do it at all.
Better lose the saddle than the horse.	It's better to stop and accept a small loss than continue and risk losing everything.

Better safe than sorry.	It's better to be too careful than to be careless and regret it later.
Better be untaught than ill-taught.	It's better not to be taught at all than to be taught badly.
Beware of Greeks bearing gifts.	Don't trust your enemies.
(A) bird in hand is worth two in a bush.	It's better to keep what you have than to risk losing it by searching for something else.
Birds of a feather flock together.	People of the same sort are usually found together.
Blood is thicker than water.	Family relationships are stronger than relationships with other people.
Blood will out.	A person's background or education will eventually show.
(A) broken friendship may be soldered but it will never be sound.	Friendships can be re built after a dispute but will never be as strong as before.
(A) burden of one's own choice is not felt.	Something difficult seems easier when it is done voluntarily.
(A) burnt child dreads the fire.	A bad experience will make people stay away from certain things.

Alphabetical List - C

(A) cat has nine lives.	Cats can survive many accidents because they land on their feet without injury. Nine lives = 3 years to play, 3 years to stray, 3 years to stay.

(A) chain is no stronger than its weakest link.	The strength of a group depends on each individual member.
(A) change is as good as a rest.	A change in routine is often as refreshing as a break or a holiday.
Charity begins at home.	A person's first duty is to help and care for his own family.
Children and fools tell the truth.	Neither children nor fools know that it is sometimes advantageous to lie.
Cleanliness is next to godliness.	A clean body is just as important as a pure soul.
Clear moon, frost soon.	If the atmosphere is clear, frost may form.
(A) closed mouth catches no flies.	If you learn when to keep silent you will avoid trouble.
Clothes don't make the man.	Appearances can be deceiving.
Constant occupation prevents temptation.	When you are busy working, you avoid temptation

Alphabetical List - D

Dead men tell no lies.	A dead person cannot cause difficulties by revealing something that it would be preferable to conceal.
Death is the great leveller.	All people are equal when they die.
Diamonds cut diamonds.	Refers to two people equally matched in wit or cunning.
Diligence is the mother of good fortune.	Hard work brings rewards.

Discretion is the better part of valour.	It is useless to take unnecessary risks.
Diseases of the soul are more dangerous than those of the body.	Thought to refer to mental and emotional disorder or spiritual torment as opposed to bodily pain.
Distance makes the heart grow fonder.	When you are separated from the person you love, your feelings are even stronger.
Dogs of the same street bark alike.	People of the same background have the same behaviour.
Don't bark if you can't bite.	Don't complain if you can't enforce your point of view.
Don't count your chickens before they're hatched.	You must not be too confident that something will be successful.
Don't dig your grave with our own knife and fork.	Don't do something yourself that causes your own downfall.
Don't judge a book by its cover.	Don't judge by appearances.
(A) dry March, a wet April and a cool May may fill barn and cellar and bring much hay.	Harvest predictions according to the weather.

Alphabetical List - E

Early to bed, and early to rise, makes a man healthy, wealthy and wise.	It is much better for you to go to bed early and to get up early in the morning;

Easier said than done.	What is suggested sounds easy, but it is more difficult to actually do it.
Elbow grease is the best polish.	Hard work gives the best results.
Empty vessels make the most noise.	The least intelligent people are often the most talkative or noisy.
(An) empty purse frigh-tens away friends.	When one's financial situation deteriorates, friends tend to disappear.
Every ass likes to hear himself bray.	People like to listen to them-selves talking.
Every cloud has a silver lining.	There is a positive or hopeful side to every situation.
Every man for himself.	You must think of your own interests before the interests of others.
Every man has his price.	Everyone's loyalty can be bought for a price.
Every man is the archi-tect of his own fortune.	Life is what you make it.
Every path has its puddle.	Progress is rarely without difficulty.
Every rose has its thorn.	Every good thing has an unpleasant side.
Every why has a where-fore.	There is an explanation for everything.
Everything in the garden is rosy.	Everything is satisfactory.
Experience is the father of wisdom.	Experience and knowledge result in better judgement.

Alphabetical List - F

Facts speak louder than words.	People show what they are really like by what they do, rather than by what they say.
Failure teaches success.	People can learn from their failures and be successful later on.
Fair exchange is no robbery.	Swapping two items of equal value is an honest deal.
False friends are worse than open enemies.	It's better to know who your real enemies are rather than trust someone who pretends to be a friend but is capable of stabbing you in the back.
Familiarity breeds contempt	Knowing someone very well can lead to a lack of respect for them.
(A) **fault confessed is half redressed.**	Confession is the beginning of forgiveness.
Fine words butter no parsnips.	No amount of talking can replace action.
First come, first served.	The first person in the line will be attended to first.
(A) flower blooms more than once.	If you miss an occasion, you can avail yourself of it another time.
(A) fly will not get into a closed mouth.	If you learn when to keep silent you will avoid trouble.
(A) fool and his money are (soon) easily parted.	A foolish person usually spends money carelessly.
(A) fool at forty is a fool forever.	If a person hasn't matured by the age of 40, they never will.

Fool me once, shame on you; fool me twice, shame on me.	One should learn from one's mistakes.
Fools rush in where angels fear to tread.	Inexperienced people become involved in situations that more intelligent people would avoid.
(A) friend to all is a friend to none.	Someone who is a friend to everyone makes none of them feel special.
(A) friend's eye is a good mirror.	A real friend will tell you the truth.
Friendship is like money, easier made than kept.	Effort is necessary to keep a friendship alive.
Friendship is love with understanding.	A friend is more tolerant than a lover/partner/spouse?

Alphabetical List - G

Gardens are not made by sitting in the shade.	Nothing is achieved without effort.
Give someone an inch and they will take a mile (or yard)	Give someone a little and they will want more - some people are never satisfied.
Give someone enough rope and they will hang themselves.	Give someone enough time and freedom and they will get into trouble.
God helps those who help themselves.	Success comes to those who make a real effort to achieve it.
Good accounting makes good friends.	You will keep your friends if you avoid disputes over money.
Good and quickly seldom meet.	A well-done job takes time.

(A) good beginning makes a good end.	If a task is carefully planned, there's a better chance that it will be well done.
(A) good conscience is a soft pillow.	You sleep well when you have nothing to feel guilty about.
(A) good mind possesses a kingdom.	Intellectual assets are more valuable than material ones.
Good management is better than good income.	Income can be lost if it is used carelessly.
Grasp all, lose all.	Trying to obtain everything will often result in gaining nothing.
Great minds think alike.	Intelligent people very often have the same idea at the same time.
Great oaks grow from small acorns.	Large successful operations can begin in a small way.
Grief divided is made lighter.	If you share your grief, it will be easier to bear.
(A) guilty conscience needs no accuser.	If you know that you have done something wrong, you don't need anyone to tell you that you're guilty.

Alphabetical List - H

Half a loaf is better than none	You should be grateful for something, even if it is not as much as you wanted.
Handsome is what handsome does.	Behaviour is more important than appearance.
Hard words breaks no bones.	Criticism or verbal attacks may be unpleasant but will not kill anyone.

Haste makes waste	If something is done too quickly, it may be done carelessly and need to be redone.
Hatred is as blind as love.	A person who feels hatred does not see any qualities in the person he/she hates.
He can who believes he can.	If you believe you can do something, you will be able to do it.
He has enough who is content.	A happy person needs nothing more.
He who hesitates is lost.	If you delay your decision too long, you may miss a good opportunity.
He who is everywhere is nowhere.	It's not good to do too many things at the same time.
He who know nothing doubts nothing.	Knowledge leads us to make choices.
He who pays the piper calls the tune.	The person who provides the money for something should control how it is spent.
He who plays with fire gets burnt.	If you behave in a risky way, you are likely to have problems.
He who wills the end wills the means.	If you are determined to do something you will find a way.
He laughs best who laughs last.	Don't express your joy, or triumph, too soon.
Health is better than wealth.	It's better to be in good health than to be rich.
(The best) helping hand is at the end of your sleeve.	The best way to get something done is to do it yourself.

Home is where the heart is.	You call home the place where the people you love are.
Honesty is the best policy.	It's always better to be honest.
Honey catches more flies than vinegar.	You can obtain more cooperation from othersby being nice.
However long the night, the dawn will break.	Bad things don't last for ever.
Hunger is a good sauce.	All food tastes good when you are hungry.

Alphabetical List - I

(An) idle brain is the devil's workshop.	When you are busy working you avoid temptation?
In times of prosperity friends are plentiful.	You have many friends when you have no difficulties.
If a camel gets his nose in a tent, his body will follow.	If you let something intrusive enter your life, your life will become difficult.
If in February there be no rain, 'tis neither good for hay nor grain.	Plants and grains will grow badly if there is no rain in early spring.
If you are patient in one moment of anger, you will avoid 100 days of sorrow.	Avoid regrets by taking the time to think before speaking or acting angrily.
If you chase two rabbits, you will not catch either one.	If you try to do two things at the same time, you will not succeed in doing either of them.
If two ride a horse, one must ride behind.	When two people do something together, one will be the leader and the other the sub-ordinate?

If you want a friend, be a friend.	Friendship must be reciprocal.
If wishes were horses, beggars would ride.	Wishing alone is of no use; you must act as well.
Ignorance is bliss.	Possible interpretation: What you do not know causes no worry or sadness?
In for a penny, in for a pound.	If you start something, it is better to spend the time or money necessary to complete it.
In the land of the blind the one-eyed man is king.	A man of even limited ability has an advantage over persons who are less able.
It never rains but it pours.	Misfortune usually comes in large numbers.
It is always darkest before the dawn.	The most difficult time is just before the problem is solved.
It's no use crying over spilt milk.	Don't express regret for something that has happened and cannot be remedied.
It takes all sorts to make a world.	People vary in character and abilities and this is a good thing.

Alphabetical List - J-K

Justice delayed is justice denied.	If the law is applied too late, it is useless.
Kill one to warn a hundred.	Warn many people by punis-hing a few.
Kill not the goose that lays the golden egg.	Do not destroy the source of your good fortune.

Kindle not a fire you cannot put out.	Do not start something that you cannot control; you may fail or cause damage.
Kindness begets kindness.	If you are kind to someone, he will return your kindness.
Knowledge in youth is wisdom in age.	What you learn when you are young, will be invaluable when you grow old.
Knowledge is power.	It is easier to make progress or be successful if you are educated or possess a lot of information.

Alphabetical List - L

Laughter is the best medicine.	Laughter makes people feel good.
Learn to walk before you run.	Don't rush into doing something before you know how to do it.
Learning is a treasure that will follow its owner everywhere.	Education is something that you keep for ever.
Least said, soonest mended.	The less you talk about an incident, the more easily it will be forgotten.
(A) leopard cannot change its spots.	It is impossible for a bad or unpleasant person to become good or pleasant.
Let bygones be bygones.	Let's forgive and forget past quarrels.
Let the chips fall where they may.	We should not try to control our destiny.
Liars need good memories.	People who do not tell the truth must be careful to remember what they say.

Lightning never strikes in the same place twice.	An unusual event is not likely to occur again in exactly the same circumstances.
Like father, like son.	A son's character can be expected to resemble his father's.
Little strokes fell good oaks.	If you divide a task into small parts, it become easier to do.
(A) loaded wagon makes no noise.	Really wealthy people do not talk about money.
Look before you leap.	Consider possible consequences before taking action.
Loose lips sink ships.	Disclosing important information (to the enemy or a competitor) could result in large losses.
Losers weepers, finders keepers.	If you lose something you lament, if you find something you keep it.
Love is blind.	A person in love does not see the faults of the person he/she loves.
(A) loveless life is a living death.	Without affection, life is difficult.

Alphabetical List - M

Make a silk purse out of a sow's ear.	Manage to product something good using poor material.
Man is the head of the family and woman is the neck that turns the head.	No comment!
Man proposes, God disposes.	Our destiny depends on God's will.

(A) man can die but once.	If death comes now, you will not have to experience it later.
(A) man is as old as he feels himself to be.	Your age doesn't matter as long as you are fit and healthy.
(A) man is known by the company he keeps.	A person's character is judged by the type of people with whom he spends his time.
Manners make the man.	Possibly: a person's manners show his origins.
Many a true word is spoken in jest.	Even if something is said as a joke it can still be true.
Many hands make light work.	Sharing work makes the task easier.
March comes in like a lion and goes out like a lamb.	The weather at the beginning of March is stormy and at the end is mild.
March winds and April showers bring forth May flowers.	The storms and rain in March and April produce flowers in the month of May.
Mark, learn and inwardly digest.	Note and reflect upon something in order to thoroughly assimilate it.
Marry in haste, repent as leisure.	If you get married too quickly, you may spend your whole life regretting it.
Memory is the treasure of the mind.	A good memory is very precious.
Men make houses, women make homes.	Women give a house its comfort and character.
Might as well be hanged for a sheep as for a lamb.	If the penalty is going to be same, you might as well commit the greater offence.

Misery loves company.	When people are sad they often like others to feel sad, too.
Money begets money.	If you have money you can make more money.
Money doesn't grow on trees.	You should not waste money because it is not obtained easily.
A monkey in silk is a monkey no less.	No matter how someone dresses, it's the same person underneath.

Alphabetical List - N

Necessity is the mother of invention.	The need for something forces people to find a way of obtaining it.
Need teaches a plan.	Necessity will make you find a solution.
Needs must when the devil drives.	Sometimes you are compelled to do something that you would rather not do.
Never put off till tom-orrow what canbe done today.	Don't postpone until later something you can do now.
Never say die.	Never give up.
Never trouble troubles until troublestrouble you.	Don't look for problems in advance; deal with them when they arise.
A new broom sweeps clean.	A newly-appointed person makes changes energetically.
Nobody is perfect.	It is understandable not to be perfect or to make occasional mistakes.
No joy without annoy.	There is no happiness without hard work.

No losers, no winners.	If there were no losers, there could be no winners.
No man can serve two masters.	It's impossible to follow instructions from two different sources.
No man is a hero to his valet.	Few people are admired by those who know them intimately and are aware of their failings.
No man is an island.	We are all inter-dependent and need other people.
No news is good news.	If the news was bad, we would hear of it. Since we have heard nothing, we can assume that all is well.
No pain, no gain.	Nothing is achieved without effort.
No rain, no grain.	Without rain the harvest will be poor.
No smoke without fire.	There could be some truth in the rumour
No wind, no waves.	Similar to 'no smoke without fire'.
Nothing ventured nothing gained.	You cannot expect to achieve anything if you take no risks.

Alphabetical List - O

Once bitten, twice shy.	After an unpleasant experience, people are careful to avoid anything similar.
One father is (worth)	A teacher cannot replace a

more than a hundred school masters.	father. A child is raised by a father and taught by a teacher.
One good turn deserves another.	You should be helpful to someone who helps you.
One of these days is none of these days.	Until a date is set, 'one of these days' remains a vague promise.
One today is worth two tomorrows.	What you have today is better than what is promised or hoped for.
One man's meat is another man's poison.	People don't always like the same things.
One man's trash is another man's treasure.	What is useless to one person could be valuable to another.
One swallow doesn't make a summer.	A single good event does not mean that all the others will be as good.
An onion a day keeps everyone away.	A humoristic version of "an apple a day..."
Only real friends will tell you when your face is dirty.	Only a real friend will tell you the truth.
Opportunity seldom knocks twice.	Don't miss the opportunities that come along.
An ounce of prevention is worth a pound of cure.	It is easier to prevent something from happening than to repair the damage or cure the disease later.
Out of the mouth of babes and sucklings.	Children often speak wisely.
Out of sight, out of mind.	We tend to forget people or things that we do not see.

Alphabetical List - P-Q

Penny wise, pound foolish.	Refers to a person who is careful about spending small amounts of money, but not careful about spending large amounts.
People who live in glass houses should not throw stones.	One should not criticize others for faults similar to one's own and risk retaliation.
Pity is akin to love.	If you begin to feel sorry for someone, you may start to love them.
Poverty waits at the gates of idleness.	If you do not work, you will not earn any money.
Practice makes perfect.	Doing something repeatedly is the only way to become good at it.
Practice what you preach.	Do yourself what you advise others to do.
Prevention is better than cure.	It is easier to prevent something from happening than to repair the damage or cure the disease later.
Pride comes before a fall.	Don't be too self-confident or proud; something may happen to make you look foolish.
A problem shared is a problem halved.	It is easier to deal with a problem when you discuss it with someone.
Procrastination is the thief of time.	Delaying an action for too long is a waste of time.

Punctuality is the soul of business.	You should always be on time for your business appointments.
Put all your eggs in one basket.	Risk everything by relying on one plan (*e.g.*, by putting all one's money into one business).

Alphabetical List - R

Revenge is sweet.	There is satisfaction in returning an injury.
(A) rising tide lifts all boats.	Refers to something that will be helpful to all.
(A) rolling stone gathers no moss	If a person keeps moving from place to place, he gains neither friends nor possessions. Another interpretation is that, by moving often, one avoids being tied down!
Rome was not built in a day.	It takes time to do a job properly. You should not expect to do it quickly.
(A) rotten apple spoils the barrel.	A dishonest or immoral person can have a bad influence on a group.

Alphabetical List - S

Save me from my friends.	Friends can be more dangerous than enemies.
Saying is one thing, doing is another.	People don't always do what they announce.
Short reckonings make long friends.	Debts paid quickly encourage friendship.

Sickness in the body brings sadness to the mind.	Physical suffering can lead to sadness or depression.
Silence gives consent.	If you don't object something, it is assumed that you agree with it.
A smooth sea never made a skilled mariner.	Overcoming adversity leads to competence.
Snug as a bug in a rug.	Feeling very comfortable.
Spare the rod and spoil the child.	If you don't punish a child when he does wrong, you will spoil his character.
Speech is silver, silence is golden.	Speaking is good, but discretion can be better.
Sticks and stones will break my bones but names will never hurt me.	Physical attacks may harm me, but cruel words will not.
Still waters run deep.	A quiet person with a calm outward appearance can have much knowledge or wisdom.
(A) stitch in time saves nine.	It's better to deal with a problem at an early stage to prevent it from getting worse.
Stolen fruit is sweet/the sweetest. Stolen pleasures are the sweetest.	What is forbidden is the most tempting.
(A) stumble may prevent a fall.	Correcting a small mistake may help you to avoid making a bigger one.
(A) swallow does not make the summer.	One good event does not mean that everything is alright.

Alphabetical List - T

Tall oaks grow from little acorns.	Great things may come from small beginnings.
The apple doesn't fall far from the tree.	Children resemble their parents.
The best advice is found on the pillow.	A good night's sleep may help us find an answer to our problem.
The best things in life are free.	You don't have to pay for what is important: Happiness, friendship, good health.
The darkest hour is just before dawn.	The most difficult moment is just before a problem is solved.
The devil looks after his own.	Success comes to those who deserve it least.
The devil makes work for idle hands.	People who have no work, or are idle, often get into trouble.
The die is cast.	A decision has been made and it is impossible to change it.
The early bird catches the worm.	If you want to do something successfully, you should do it as soon as you can.
The end justifies the means.	Wrong or unfair methods may be used if the result of the action is good.
The first step is the hardest.	The most difficult part of an action is the beginning.
The more haste, the less speed.	A person makes more progress if they take time to do things carefully.
The more you have, the more you want.	People have a constant desire to possess more.

The mouse that has but one hole isquickly taken.	If you depend on just one thing, and it fails, you have no alternatives.
The pen is mightier than the sword.	Words and communication have a greater effect than war and fighting.
The proof of the pudding is in the eating.	The real value of something can be judged only after it has been tried or tested.
The road to hell is paved with good intentions.	It is not enough to intend to do something, you must actually do it.
The tongue wounds more than a lance.	Insults can be more hurtful than physical injuries.
The truth is in the wine.	People speak more freely under the influence of alcohol.
The wish is father to the thought.	You think that something is true because you want it to be so.
There is a black sheep in every flock.	There is always someone who doesn't behave or perform like the others.
There's many a slip between the cupand the lip.	We do not own something until we actually get it.
There is a trick in every trade.	There is an established way of doing things.
There is no fool like an old fool.	An older person is expected to behave more sensibly.
There is safety in numbers.	Being in a crowd makes you feel more confident.
Time and tide wait for no man.	Delaying a decision will not prevent events from taking place.

Time has wings.	Time goes by quickly.
Time heals all wounds.	The passage of time lessens the impact of bad events.
Time is money.	Time is valuable and should not be wasted.
To err is human, to forgive divine.	It is human nature to make mistakes, therefore, one should forgive them.
Too many cooks spoil the broth.	If too many people are involved in something, it will not be done properly.
Too much bed makes a dull head.	When you sleep too much, you are not able to think clearly.
A tree is known by its fruit.	A person is judged by their actions.
Trust not a horse's heel nor a dog'stooth.	A horse kicks from behind, a dog attacks with its teeth.
Truth has no answer.	You cannot argue against facts or refute what is true.
Truth is stranger than fiction.	Events in real life are often stranger than in fiction.
Two wrongs don't make a right.	It is wrong to harm someone because they have harmed you.

Alphabetical List - U-V

Union is strength	A group has more force than an individual.
Unwillingness easily finds an excuse.	A person who doesn't want to do something always finds a reason to avoid it.

Variety is the spice of life.	Doing a lot of different things makes life more interesting.
Virtue is its own reward.	You should not expect praise for acting in a correct or moral way.

Alphabetical List - W

Walls have ears.	Be careful. People could be listening.
Waste not, want not.	If you never waste anything, you will have it when you need it.
A watched pot never boils.	If you wait anxiously for something to happen, it seems to take a long time.
What the eye doesn't see, the heart doesn't grieve over.	If a person doesn't know about something, it cannot hurt them.
What a man says drunk, he thinks sober.	People speak more freely under the influence of alcohol.
What soberness conceals, drunkenness reveals.	People are less discreet under the influence of alcohol.
When the cat's away, the mice play.	People sometimes misbehave when the person in authority, is absent.
When in Rome, do as the Romans do.	You should adopt the customs of the people or country you are visiting and behave in the same way.
When poverty comes in the door, love goes out the window.	When a couple loses everything, their relationship becomes difficult.
Where there's life there's hope.	As long as a person is breathing, there is hope for recovery.

Where there's a will there's a way.	If you are determined to do something, you will find a way to do it.
Who makes himself a sheep will be eaten by the wolves.	Possible interpretation: an easily influenced person can be mislead.
Wisdom is better than strength.	It is preferable to use one's intelligence than one's physical strength.
Wonders will never cease!	Expresses surprise at an unexpected pleasure or event.
Worry often gives a small thing a big shadow.	Worrying over small details can make them seem worse.

Alphabetical List - X-Y-Z

You are what you eat.	What you eat has an effect on your well-being.
You are never too old to learn.	You can always learn something new, no matter how old you are.
You can lead a horse to water but you can't make it drink.	You can offer somebody an opportunity to do something but you can't force them to do it.
You can't teach an old dog new tricks.	A person who is used to doing things a certain way cannot change.
You never know what you can do until you try.	Try first before deciding not to do something.
You scratch my back and I'll scratch yours.	You help me and I'll help you.
(A) young idler, an old beggar.	If you don't work, you won't have any money when you're old.

FAMOUS QUOTATIONS

Quotation - A

	Author
"After all is said and done, more is said than done."	Aesop
"When I was born, I was so surprised I didn't talk for a year and a half."	Gracie Allen
"I'm not afraid to die. I just don't want to be there when it happens."	Woody Allen
"The secret of life is not to do what you like, but to like what you do."	Anonymous
"A real friend is someone who walks in when the rest of the world walks out"	Anonymous
"Opportunity may knock only once, but temptation leans on the doorbell."	Anonymous
"Good supervision is the art of getting average people to do superior work."	Anonymous
"Wit is educated insolence."	Aristotle
"Education is the best provision for the journey to old age."	Aristotle
"One swallow does not make the spring."	Aristotle
"Pleasure in the job puts perfection in the work."	Aristotle
"We are what we repeatedly do."	Aristotle
"Wishing to be friends is quick work, but friendship is a slow ripening fruit."	Aristotle
"There is safety in numbers."	Anonymous

Quotation - B

	Author
"Thc worst solitude is to be destitute of sincere friendship."	Sir Francis **B**acon
"Knowledge is power."	Sir Francis **B**acon
"Behind every great fortune there is a crime."	Honore de **B**alzac
"An error doesn't become a mistake until you refuse to correct it."	Orlando A; **B**attisa
"There is no such thing as a long piece of work, except one that you dare not start.	Charles **B**audelaire
"When one door closes, another opens; but we often look so long and so regretfully upon the closed door that we do not see the one which has opened for us."	Alexander Graham **B**ell
"Happiness lies in good health and a bad memory."	Ingrid **B**ergman
"Only a fool learns from his own mistakes. The wise man learns from the mistakes of others.	Otto von **B**ismarck
"Ability is nothing without opportunity."	Napoleon **B**onaparte
"Glory is fleeting but obscurity is forever."	Napoleon **B**onaparte
"Never interrupt your enemy when he is making a mistake."	Napoleon **B**onaparte
"The heart has reasons that reason does not understand."	Jacques **B**ossuet

Quotation - C

	Author
"Never stand begging for that which you have the power to earn."	Miguel de Cervantes
"There are people who have money and people who are rich."	Coco Chanel
"Don't ever take a fence down until you know the reason it was put up."	G.K.Chesterton
"A woman used her intelligence to find reasons to support her intuition."	G.K.Chesterton
"We make a living by what we get. We make a life by what we give."	Winston Churchill
"A pessimist sees the difficulty in every opportunity; an optimist sees the opportunity in every difficulty."	Winston Churchill
"Success is the ability to go from one failure to another with no loss of enthusiasm."	Winston Churchill
"If you are going through hell, keep going."	Winston Churchill
"History will be kind to me for I intend to write it."	Winston Churchill
"A lie gets halfway around the world before the truth has a chance to get its pants on."	Winston Churchill
"The price of greatness is responsibility."	Winston Churchill
"Out of intense complexities, intense simplicities emerge."	Winston Churchill
"Gratitude is not only the greatest of virtues, but the parent of all others."	Cicero

"Progress is the injustice each generation commits with regard to its predecessors."	E.M.Cioran
"I believe in luck; how else can you explain the success of those you dislike?"	Jean Cocteau
"Choose a job you love and you will never have to work a day in your life.	Conficius
"Our greatest glory is not in never falling, but in rising every time we fall."	Conficius
"Respect yourself and others will respect you."	Conficius
"The superior man is slow in his words and earnest in his conduct."	Conficius
"Nothing in life is to be feared; it is only to be understood."	Marie Curie

Quotation - D

Author	
"The only difference between me and amadman is that I'm not mad."	Salvador Dali
"Have no fear of perfection; you'll never reach it."	Salvador Dali
"It is not the strongest of the species that survives, nor the most intelligent, but the one most responsive to change."	Charles Darwin
"It's the friends you can call up at 4 a.m. that matter."	Marlene Dietrich
"Talk to a man about himself and he will listen for hours."	Benjamin Disraeli
"The greatest good you can do for another is not just share your riches, but reveal to him his own."	Benjamin Disraeli

"There are three kinds of lies: lies, damned lies and statistics."	Benjamin Disraeli
"Little things affect little minds."	Benjamin Disraeli
"My idea of an agreeable person is a person who agrees with me."	Benjamin Disraeli
"The secret of success is constancy of purpose."	Benjamin Disraeli
"Pure love and suspicion cannot dwell together; at the door where the latter enters, the former makes its exit.	Alexandre Dumas
"All for one and one for all."	Alexandre Dumas

Quotation - E

Author	
"Genius is one percent inspiration and ninety-nine percent perspiration."	Thomas Edison
"Only two things are infinite - the universe and human stupidity and I'm not sure about the former."	Albert Einstein
"When you are courting a nice girl, an hour seems like a second. When you sit on a red-hot cinder, a second seems like an hour. That's relativity."	Albert Einstein
"Not everything that can be counted counts and not everything that counts can be counted."	Albert Einstein
"The difference between genius and stupidity is that genius has its limits."	Albert Einstein
"It's not that I'm so smart, it's just that I stay with problems longer."	Albert Einstein
"Anyone who has never made a mistake has never tried anything new."	Albert Einstein

"Before God we are all equally wise- and equally foolish."	Albert Einstein
"Great spirits have always encountered violent opposition from mediocre minds."	Albert Einstein
"Gravitation cannot be held responsible for people falling in love."	Albert Einstein
"I never think of the future. It comes soon enough."	Albert Einstein
"The only way to have a friend is to be one."	Ralph Waldo Emerson
"In case of dissension, never dare to judge till you've heard the other side."	Euripedes
"Man's best possession is a sympathetic wife."	Euripedes

Quotation - F

Author	
"A writer is congenitally unable to tell the truth, and that is why we call what he writes fiction."	William Faulkner
"A business that makes nothing but money is a poor kind of business."	Henry Ford
"Obstacles are those frightful things you see when you take your eyes off your goal."	Henry Ford
"You can't build a reputation on what you are going to do."	Henry Ford
"The biggest mistake people make in life is not trying to make a living at doing what they most enjoy."	Malcolm Forbes
"To accomplish great things, we must not only act but also dream; not only plan but also believe."	Anatole France

"Admiration is the daughter of ignorance."	Benjamin Franklin
"Most fools think they are only ignorant."	Benjamin Franklin
"Blessed is he who expects nothing, for he shall never be disappointed."	Benjamin Franklin
"Creative minds have always been known to survive any kind of bad training."	Anna Freud
"Men are more moral than they think, and far more immoral that they can imagine."	Sigmund Freud

Quotation - G

Author	
"We cannot teach people anything; we can only help them discover it within themselves."	Galileo Gallilei
"I believe in equality for everyone, except reporters and photographers."	Mahatma Gandhi
"You must be the change you wish to see in the world."	Mahatma Gandhi
"Live as if you were to die tomorrow; learn as if you were to live forever."	Mahatma Gandhi
"Don't let yourself be lulled into inaction."	Bill Gates
"Nothing strengthens authority as much as silence."	Charles de Gaulle
"Graveyards are full of indispensable men."	Charles de Gaulle
"Formula for success : Rise early, work hard, strike oil."	J. Paul Getty

"Money isn't everything but it sure keeps you in touch with your children"	J. Paul Getty
"If you can actually count your money then you are not a rich man."	J. Paul Getty
"All the world over I will back the masses against the classes."	William Gladstone
"Enjoy when you can and endure when you must."	J.W. van Goethe
"Knowing is not enough; we must apply. Willing is not enough; we must do."	J.W. van Goethe
"Whatever you can do or dream, begin it."	J.W. van Goethe
"A man can stand anything except a succession of ordinary days."	J.W. van Goethe
"Talent develops in tranquillity, character in the full current of human life."	J.W. van Goethe

<u>Quotation - H</u>

Author	
"Never confuse movement with action."	Ernest Hemmingway
"There is no better friend than a book."	Ernest Hemmingway
"Drama is life with the dull bits cut out."	Alfred Hitchcock
"Seize the day, put no trust in tomorrow."	Horace
"Forty is the old age of youth; fifty is the youth of old age."	Victor Hugo
"Life is the flower for which love is the honey."	Victor Hugo
"Intelligence is the wife, imagination is the mistress, memory is the servant."	Victor Hugo

"Experience is not what happens to a man. It is what a man does with what happens to him."	Aldous **H**uxley
"Maybe this world is another planet's hell."	Aldous **H**uxley

Quotation - J

Author	
"In matters of style, swim with the current, in matters of principle, stand like a rock."	Thomas **J**efferson
"Our brightest blazes are commonly kindled by unexpected sparks."	Samuel **J**ohnson
"When making your choices in life, do not forget to live."	Samuel **J**ohnson
"Love is the wisdom of the fool and the folly of the wise."	

Quotation - K

Author	
"Science is organized knowledge. Wisdom is organized life."	Immanuel **K**ant
"Forgive your enemies, but never forget their names."	John F. **K**ennedy
"When written in Chinese, the word crisis is composed of two characters. One represents danger, the other represents opportunity."	John F. **K**ennedy
"Man is still the most extraordinary computer of all."	John F. **K**ennedy
"Liberty without learning is always in peril; learning without liberty is always in vain."	John F. **K**ennedy

"Education : the inculcation of the incomprehensible into the indifferent by the incompetent.	John Maynard **K**eynes
"In the end we will remember not the words of our enemies but the silence of our friends."	Martin Luther **K**ing
"Take everything you like seriously, except yourselves."	Rudyard **K**ipling
"Gardens are not made by sitting in the shade."	Rudyard **K**ipling
"The absence of alternatives clears the mind marvellously."	Henry **K**issinger
"The nice thing about being a celebrity is that if you bore people they think it's their fault."	Henry **K**issinger

Quotation - L

Author	
"We can live without religion and meditation, but we cannot survive without human affection."	Dalai **L**ama
"Life is what happens when you are busy making other plans."	John **L**ennon
"In the end it's not the years in your life that count, it's the life in your years."	Abraham **L**incoln
"Nearly all men can stand adversity, but if you want to test a man's character, give him power."	Abraham **L**incoln
"You cannot escape the responsibility of tomorrow by evading it today."	Abraham **L**incoln

"You can fool all of the people some of the time, and some of the people all of the time, but you can't fool all of the people all of the time."	Abraham Lincoln

Quotation - M

Author	
"No enterprise is more likely to succeed than one concealed from the enemy until it is ripe for execution."	Niccolo Machiavelli
"People ask for criticism, but they only want praise."	Somerset Maugham
"It is cruel to discover one's mediocrity only when it is too late."	Somerset Maugham
"The greater the obstacle, the more glory in overcoming it."	Moliere
"To the soul there is hardly anything more healing than friendship."	

Quotation - N

Author	
"Tact is the knack of making a point without making an enemy."	Isaac Newton
"The advantage of a bad memory is that one enjoys several times the same good things for the first time."	Friedrich Nietzsche
"What doesn't kill you will make you stronger."	Friedrich Nietzsche
"When one has much to put into them, a day has a hundred pockets."	Friedrich Nietzsche
"We don't see things as they are; we see things as we are."	Anais Nin

"Life shrinks or expands in proportion to one's courage."	Anais **N**in

Quotation - O

Author	
"Burdens become light when cheerfully borne."	Ovid

Quotation - P

Author	
"In the field of observation, chance favours only the prepared mind."	Louis **P**asteur
"The chief enemy of creativity is good taste."	Pablio **P**icasso
"The mind is not a vessel to be filled but a fire to be kindled."	**P**lutarch
"Fools rush in where angels fear to tread."	Alexander **P**ope
"The voyage to discovery is not in seeking new landscapes but in having new eyes."	Marcel **P**roust

Quotation - R

Author	
"If you wish to avoid seeing a fool, you must break your mirror."	Francois **R**abelais
"A statesman is a successful politician who is dead."	Thomas Brackett **R**eed
"The customer is never wrong."	Cesar **R**itz
"Instruction ends in the school room, but education ends only with life."	F.W. **R**obertson

"Many people despise wealth but few know how to give it away."	F. de la **R**ochefoucauld
"Men give away nothing so liberally as their advice."	F. de la **R**ochefoucauld
"No one can make you feel inferior without your consent."	Eleanor **R**oosevelt
"The only thing we have to fear is fear itself."	Franklin D. **R**oosevelt
"Rules are not necessarily sacred; principles are."	Franklin D. **R**oosevelt
"I ask you to judge me by the enemies I have made."	Franklin D. **R**oosevelt
"The only man who never makes mistakes is the man who never does anything."	Theodore **R**oosevelt
"If it can't be cured it must be endured."	Salman **R**ushdie
"When love and skill work together, expect a masterpiece."	John **R**uskin

Quotation - S

Author	
"Perfection is achieved, not when there is nothing more to add, but when there is nothing left to take away."	Antoine de **S**t Exupery
"Life has taught us that love does not consist in gazing at each other but in looking outward together in the same direction.	Antoine de **S**t Exupery
"Hell is other people."	Jean-Paul **S**artre
"It is wise to learn; it is God-like to create."	John **S**axe

"For success, attitude is equally as important as ability."	Sir Walter Scott
"Luck is what happens when preparation meets opportunity."	Lucius Annaeus Seneca
"Life is a play. It's not its length but its performance that counts."	Lucius Annaeus Seneca
"Action is eloquence."	William Shakespeare
"All that glitters is not gold."	William Shakespeare
"Our bodies are our gardens to which our wills are gardeners."	William Shakespeare
"Great Britain and the United States are nations separated by a common language."	George Bernard Shaw
"The greatest of our evils and the worst of our crimes is poverty."	George Bernard Shaw
Youth is a wonderful thing. What a crime to waste it on children!"	George Bernard Shaw
"Martyrdom ... is the only way in which a man can become famous without ability."	George Bernard Shaw
"We don't stop playing because we grow; we grow old because we stop playing."	George Bernard Shaw
"Reasonable men adapt to the world. Unreasonable men adapt the world to themselves. That's why all progress depends on unreasonable men."	George Bernard Shaw
"Can a man who is warm understand one who is freezing?"	Alexander Solzhenitsyn

"Don't judge each day by the harvest you reap ... but by the seeds you plant!"	Robert Louis Stevenson
"Politics is perhap the only profession for which no preparation is thought necessary."	Robert Louis Stevenson
"Vision is the art of seeing things invisible.	Jonathan Swift
"May you live every day of your life."	Jonathan Swift

Quotation - T

Author	
"I am more afraid of an army of a hundred sheep led by a lion, than by an army of a hundred lions led by a sheep."	Talleyrand
"'Tis better to have loved and lost than never to have loved at all."	Alfred Lord Tennyson
"A good laugh is sunshine in a house."	William Thackery
"Love is real only when a person can sacrifice himself for another."	Leo Tolstoy
"It is better to keep your mouth closed and let people think you are a fool than to open it and remove all doubt."	Mark Twain
"Be careful of reading health books. You may die of a misprint."	Mark Twain
"Wrinkles should merely indicate where smiles have been."	Mark Twain

Quotation - U

Author	
"The only thing in life achieved without effort is failure."	Unknown

"The speed of the leader determines the rate of the pack."	Unknown
"Many receive advice; only the wise profit from it."	Unknown
"Remember, no one can make you feel inferior without your consent."	Unknown
"Genius is the ability to reduce the complicated to the simple."	Unknown
"The secret of happiness is not doing what one likes, but in liking what one does."	Unknown
"Only those who keep trying eventually win."	Unknown
"Getting something done is an accomplishment; getting something done right is an achievement."	Unknown
"Do not let what you cannot do interfere with what you can do."	Unknown
"The best time to do something worthwhile is between yesterday and tomorrow."	Unknown

Quotation - V

Author	
"Conscience is a man's compass."	Vinvent Van Gogh
"The progress of rivers to the ocean is not as rapid as that of man to error."	Voltaire
"Anything that is too stupid to be spoken is sung."	Voltaire
"God is a comedian playing to an audience too afraid to laugh."	Voltaire

"The greatest consolation in life is to say what one thinks."	Voltaire
"Doubt is not an agreeable condition, but certainty is an absurd one."	Voltaire
"The secret of being a bore is to tell everything."	Voltaire
"Think for yourself and let others enjoy the privilege of doing so too."	Voltaire

Quotation - W

	Author
"The only way to get rid of a temptation is to get rid of it."	Oscar Wilde
"Some cause happiness wherever they go; others whenever they go."	Oscar Wilde
"My own business always bores me to death; I prefer other people's."	Oscar Wilde
"Experience is the name so many people give to their mistakes."	Oscar Wilde
"Wisdom is knowing how little we know."	Oscar Wilde
"To live is the rarest thing in the world. Most people exist, that's all."	Oscar Wilde
"The old believe everything, the middle-aged suspect everything, the young know everything."	Oscar Wilde
"No man is rich enough to buy back his past."	Oscar Wilde
"There are only two tragedies in life : one is not getting what one wants, the other is getting it."	Oscar Wilde

"True friends stab you in the front."	Oscar **W**ilde
"Fashion is a form of ugliness so intolerable that we have to alter it every six months."	Oscar **W**ilde
"All cruel people describe themselves as paragons of frankness."	Tennessee **W**illiams

Quotation - Y

Author	
"Education is not the filling of a pail but rather the lighting of a fire."	William Butler **Y**eats

Quotation - Z

Author	
"The artist is nothing without the gift, but the gift is nothing without work."	Emile **Z**ola

Chapter 2-CONFIDENCE BUILDING

CURBING FEAR

FEAR can only be overcome through continuous practice and proper preparation.

A certain amount of stage fright is useful. It is nervous energy. If controlled and properly channeled it is a strength and vigor – an asset.

HOW TO TRUN NERVOUSNESS INTO AN ASSET

- Accept your fears.
- Analyze your fears: Real, imaginary or based on some past experience.
- Avoid visions of doom and gloom
- Get involved–think positive
- Persistence

Non Verbal Actions which assist Communication

- Maintaining eye contact
- Occasionally nodding the head in agreement.
- Smiling and showing animation
- Speaking at a moderate rate in a positive tone.

Psychological Aspects

1. Lack of consideration for other's feelings.
2. Difference in perception
3. Lack of knowledge

4. Lack of interest
5. Aggressiveness
6. Threat of fear

- The main enemy of a presenter is tension, which ruins the voice, posture and spontaneity.
- The voice becomes higher as the throat tenses.
- Shoulders tighten up and limit flexibility while the legs start to shake and cause unsteadiness.
- The presentation becomes "canned" as the speaker locoks in on the notes and starts to read directly from them.
- First, do not fight nerves, welcome them! Then you can get on with the presentation instead of focusing in on being nervous.
- Your body communicates different impressions to the audience. People not only listen to you, they also watch you.
- Slouching tells them you are indifferent or you do not care even though you might care a great deal!
- On the other hand, displaying good posture tells your audience that you know what you are doing and you care deeply about it. Also, a good posture helps you to speak more clearly and effectively.

Self Motivation

This is central to everything positive that you want to do in your life. Perhaps it is even more important than your self esteem!

Why?

Because if you want to improve your self-esteem or improve yourself in any way at all you first need the inner desire and will to do it.

Why you need self motivation?

- You cannot always rely on others to encourage you, if you have positive friends who are always there when you need them then you are indeed lucky and very much in the minority.
- If you are lonely or have few friends when you face any difficulties in your life you must rely on your own motivation to get you through. Lack of self-motivation at that time could lead to depression.
- You need self-motivation to achieve because if you don't encourage yourself to accept opportunity and challenge, who will?
- To plan and find direction in your life.
- To take up a new activity, hobby or challenge.
- To be enthusiastic about life and living.
- To have the courage to see things through despite setbacks or negative comments from others.

What if you lack self-motivation?

- Focus on what you really enjoy doing, maybe on something you want to take up or on a hobby you've always wanted to devote more time to. What's stopping you? Think about giving it priority to start doing what you love doing.
- Make a list of things you'd like to improve on and how you're going to do it.
- Review all the successes you've enjoyed in every area of your life, totally forget any negatives, just positive successes here!
- Start an exercise program - force yourself to do it, it'll make you feel much more positive.
- Contact a positive friend and have a chat.

- Read inspiring books that will help heal your mind and improve your attitude.
- Before the presentation, visualize the room, audience and you giving the presentation. Mentally go over what you are going to do from the moment you start to the end of the presentation.
- During the presentation: Take a moment to yourself by getting a drink of water, take a deep breath, concentrate on relaxing the most tense part of your body and then return to the presentation saying to your self...................

I CAN DO IT

Chapter 3-PRONUNCIATION

When speaking, pronunciation plays a very important role as it enhances the power of speech:

When learning, pronunciation we need to not only focus on syllables (word-sound parts) but also on intonation as it enhances our skills.

Every sound of every language is within every child, but as we grow we get enveloped in our comfort zones and stop listening to different sounds. Phonetics teaches us how to use our sounds right and hence, develop a neutralized accent which is far from regional.So let's begin.......

Things to Remember

- Until you learn correct English, slow down your speech.
- It is very important that everything you say is understood.
- Use your dictionary. Make a list of frequently used words that are difficult for you to pronounce.
- Record yourself your reading some sections of a book.
- Pronounce the endings of each word. Pay special stress to "s" and "ed" endings.
- Read aloud in English 15-20 minutes everyday.
- Speak with energy and enthusiasm.

- Change your body language .
- Be Patient–You can change the way you speak but it won't happen overnight!
- Always Remember

"It's not what you say but how you say it that counts."

Consonant Sounds

To begin with consonant sounds you need to remember that:–

- There are 5 vowels in English language and the rest 21 alphabets are consonants.
- Consonant sounds are produced with an obstruction or a complete closure in the vocal tract. *e.g.*/t//g//s.

Rules to Remember

- *T*–Words starting with T should sound crisp.
- *e.g.* :Ted,Toy,Tokyo, Today, Tuesday
- *F*–Bite your lip when you say words starting with F.
- *e.g.* :Few, Feather, Fine, Fun.
- *W*–Make a whistle with your mouth and then pull it back.
- *e.g.*: Washington,Weather,Why,Woman.

The Sound of 'P'

Pat's Patched Hat

Pat had a patched hat. The patches were in pink and purple. But Pat thought that the patches were not pretty enough. Pat decided to make it more pretty. He had a whole pile of pinky, punkythoughts, but didn't know how to pile them.

The 'W' sound

Whether the Weather

Whether the weather be fine
Whether the weather be not
Whether the weather be cold
Whether the weather be hot.
We'll weather the weather
Whatever the weather
Whether we like it or not.

Thumbelina

Once upon a time there lived a girl named Thumbelina, who was as small as a thumb. There were thousands and thousands of people who adored Thumbelina.

The little girl who was as small as a thumb, was thin and thoroughly well mannered. One day when she was playing in the thick grass she got thoroughly lost.

She was rather glad that she was lost; that way she knew that she would not be bothered. But that could not happen as there was thorough search and she was found.

Vowel Sounds

In English there are 5 vowels:

a, e, i, o, u

The sound which is emitted when we say a word with a vowel is called a vowel sound.

e.g. Beat

The vowels "ea" are in the middle.

When we say Beat, the sound in the middle is "ee" which is a vowel sound.

Vowel sounds are divided into 2 categories based on their sound:–

- Long Vowel Sound
- Short Vowel Sound

Long vowel sounds are stretched sounds whereas short vowel sounds are clipped sounds.

Long Vowel Sound

EE	**OO**	**AH**	**AWW**	**ER**
Beat	Boot	Bath	Born	Burp
Cheek	Cooed	Cart	Corn	Curd
Deal	Drool	Dart	Dawn	Dirt
Feel	Fool	Far	Borrow	Burn
Greed	Who	Grass	Glory	Girl
Heat	Juice	Heart	Horse	Hirsute
Jeans	Cool	Jar	Jaunt	Germ
Key	Moose	Calm	Call	Worm
Meek	Pool	Mass	Morning	Lurk
Neil	Tool	Nazi		Mirth
Peel	Stool	Pass	Pour	Pearl

Short Vowel Sound

eh	**i**	**oo**	**uh**	**aw**
Bet	Bit	Book	But	Baught
Check	Chick	Cook	Cut	Caught
Desk	Did	Push	Does	Dot
Debt	Fit	Foot	Fun	Frock
Fence	Grit	Good	Gut	Got
Get	Kill	Took	Cud	Cot

Ked	Lit	Look	Lump	Lottery
Let	Milk	Should	Muck	Mock
Men	Knit	Nook	Knuckle	Knock
Pet	Pit	Put	Putt	Poporn
Said	Pick	Pull	Shut	Proper

Understanding Intonation

Intonation is the combination of pitch, tone, volume and inflection in our voice. When we speak we sound very dull because of lack of intonation and rhythm in our speech.

√ Pitch–The shrillness of the voice is called pitch.

√ Tone–Refers to the attitude with which we speak. It reflects our inner thoughts.

√ Volume–Is the increase and decrease in sound

√ Inflection–The change in meaning of a sentence when we stress on different words.

Guidelines for Practicing Intonation

1. Pause between sentences.
2. Raise your pitch and loudness at the end of yes/no questions.

   e.g.:Are you going to the market?

   Are you a ghost?
3. Drop your pitch and loudness at the end of a default statement.

   e.g.:It is great working with your company.

   I am feeling good today.

Pronouncing the Consonants

- A–Aey J-jhay
- B–Bee K–Kay

- C–See
- D–Dee
- F–Ehf
- G–Gee
- H–Aitch
- R–Are
- S–Ess
- T–Thi
- V–We
- W–Dubyu
- X–Ex
- Y–Why
- Z–Zee

L–Elle
M–Emme
N–Enne
P–Phi
Q–Queue

Reading Lines for Pronunciation Practice

1. Have you ever fallen flat on your back because of ice?
2. In winter, it is so easy to slip when the streets get coated with a layer of show. It is especially easy if you do not live in a place that has harsh winters. In that case, you wouldn't have the right shoes.
3. A lot of people get small injuries because they fall so hard when they slip. Sometimes these injuries take months or even years to heal completely.
4. One time, I slipped and fell flat on my back. For some minutes I could not move. At first, I could not breathe.
5. Soon I was O.K. I was only twenty-two, so my bones healed easily.
6. Now I am very careful when it is showy. And I have a pair of good shoes for those days

1. My mom drove me to school fifteen minutes late on Tuesday.
2. The girl wore her hair in two braids, tied with two blue bows.
3. The mouse was so hungry, he ran across the kitchen floor without even looking for humans.
4. The tape got stuck on my lips, so I couldn't talk anymore.
5. The door slammed down on my hand and I screamed like a little baby.
6. My shoes are blue with yellow stripes and green stars on the front.
7. The mailbox was bent and broken and looked like someone had knocked it over on purpose.
8. I was so thirsty I couldn't wait to get a drink of water.
9. I found a gold coin on the playground after school today.
10. The chocolate chip cookies smelled so good that I ate one without asking.
11. My bandaid wasn't sticky any more, so it fell off on the way to school.
12. He had a sore throat so I gave him my bottle of water and told him to keep it.
13. The church was white and brown and looked very old.
14. I was so scared to go to a monster movie but my dad said he would sit with me, so we went last night.
15. Your mom is so nice, she gave me a ride home today.

16. I fell in the mud when I was walking home from school today.
17. This dinner is so delicious, I can't stop eating.
18. The school principal was so mean that all the children were scared of him.
19. I went to the dentist the other day and he let me pick a prize out of the prize box.
20. The box was small and wrapped in paper with tiny silver and red glitter dots.
21. My dad is so funny that he told us jokes all night long and we never fell asleep.
22. The camping trip was so awesome that I didn't want to come home.
23. Are you going to have a blue birthday cake for your next birthday?
24. How did you know that I was going to have a peanut butter sandwich for lunch?
25. That boy is so mean that he doesn't care if a door slams in your face or if he cuts in line.
26. The moms and dads all sat around drinking coffee and eating donuts.
27. My mom made a milkshake with frozen bananas and chocolate sauce.
28. My pen broke and leaked blue ink all over my new dress.
29. I got my haircut today and they did it way too short.
30. My pet turtle, Jim, got out of his cage and I could not find him anywhere.
31. The dog was so tired he, fell asleep on the way to his doghouse.

32. My mom drives a green jeep and my dad drives a black truck.
33. Your sister is my best friend because she always shares her treats with me.
34. My pet Roger is white and fluffy and he loves to eat carrots.
35. Your neighbour is annoying because he cut down my trees.
36. The tape was so sticky it got stuck to my fingers and wouldn't come off.
37. My glass of water broke when it fell off the table.
38. The clock was ticking and kept me awake all night.
39. My dad told me that I was his favourite person in the whole wide world.
40. The chickens were running around and pecking worms out of the ground.
41. The game looked fun but all the pieces were missing.
42. I got my finger stuck in the door when I slammed it.
43. I was so mad that I yelled at him at the top of my lungs.
44. My favourite dress is ruined because I spilled ketchup on it last night.
45. My home is bright pink and has yellow flowers growing all around it.
46. My buddy is going to pick me up after school and give me a ride to work.
47. I don't know where my friends went to invite them to my birthday party.
48. The gum was stuck under the desk and I couldn't get it off.

49. The baby was so cute but she was crying so loud, I had to plug my ears.
50. The flowers smelled beautiful and made the room so happy.
51. My sister likes to eat cheese on her peanut butter sandwich and pickles on her ice cream.
52. The alligator's teeth were so scary that I ran back to the car as fast as I could.
53. Her dress was blue with white and pink polka dots
54. The puzzle took me so long to put together that I threw it in the garbage.
55. He was driving me crazy, so I told a joke and made him laugh.
56. I started walking home and my feet got so tired I had to stop and take breaks.
57. I piled my books in my arms and they fell all over the floor.
58. The dog chased the cat around the block 4 times.
59. My lunch box had a peanut butter sandwich, crackers, juice, and a cheese stick in it.
60. I accidently left my money in my pants pocket and it got ruined in the washer.

Reading Passages

He came into the room, looked at the disorder and was perplexed. How it came to be like this he could not imagine. The silence was broken. He waited anxiously for some sign of life. Nothing at all. His eyes moved furtively from wall to door , from floor to ....corner.... There in the corner, slumped between overturned chairs was a man, face drained to a pallor and still a lifeless creature. There was no phone in the house, no means of contact with the outside world. There was nothing to be done but to leave immediately and run, run as fast as he could, away from the disorder, away from the chaos, away from responsibility. Tell no one, get away, far away, run, run, fast, faster, feet moving, feet, feet, out of step not my step, step another step, louder, nearer, quicker, thus, thud, stop.

Read these sentences with the "T" sound for "ed:"

1. The man clocked in at 10 a.m.
2. She laughed for a long time.
3. The old interstate bridged the river.
4. We stopped at the traffic light.
5. The boy tossed the pizza over and over again.
6. We were jazzed about the new dance hall.
7. They washed their hands.

Read these sentences with the "ed" sound:

1. The criminal was in a padded cell.
2. The baseball player batted very well last year.
3. The couple was wedded on January 26th.
4. She fretted until she found a good lawyer.

Read these sentences with the "D" sound for "ed:"

1. Ducks have webbed feet.
2. The boy bagged my groceries.
3. Our car was jammed between two Mac trucks.
4. The old woman fanned herself all night.
5. When the lion roared, the eagle soared.

6. They vowed to stay together for ever.
7. Roads are paved with good intentions.
8. The man stayed home all day.

List of Mispronounced Words

Didn't	dint
Representative	rep-rhey-zent-titive
Regime	rhe-zhime
Schedule	skhey-jule
Psychology	sai-kaww-lagy
Photography	futo-grufy
Biology	bye-aww-lagy
Forget	fuh-get
Pronunciation	pruh-nun-see-eh-shan
Probably	praww-bub-lee
Partial	pahr-shial
Precious	preh-shious
Project(n)	praww-ject
Pizza	peedza
Engage	en-gage
Enjoy	in-joy
Government	gah-vament
Monotony	man-aww-tuny
Address(n)	add-ress
Colony	caww-luny
Balcony	bahl-cuny
American	a-merry-kan

the "T" sound	the "ed" sound	the "D" sound
c/k, f (gh or ph), j, (dge), p, s, z, sh, ch	d, t	b, g, l, m, n, r, w, v, y, a, e, i, o, u
Asked	accepted	agreed
Changed	acted	believed
Developed	admitted	called
Finished	decided	carried
Helped	expected	explained
Introduced	included	followed
Liked	indicated	happened
Promised	lasted	learned
Reached	needed	lived
Stopped	reported	listened
Talked	started	played
Walked	suggested	remembered
Washed	tested	seemed
Watched	waited	showed
Worked	wanted	Travelled

Medial zh by Syllables

Words are divided by clearcut sounds called syllables. Here, are a few such words; hyphens indicate sounds.

2 Syllables	3 Syllables	4 Syllables
A-sia	am-ne-sia	a-ccu-sa-tion
a-zure	a-pha-sia	ca-su-a-lly
clo-sure	a-ver-sion	dis-i-llu-sion
Hoo-sier	ca-sual	mea-sure-a-ble
lei-sure	cau-ca-sian	mea-su-ring cup

mea-sure	co-lli-sion	mea-su-ring tape
Per-sia	com-po-sure	plea-su-ra-ble
plea-sure	con-clu-sion	sub-di-vi-sion
sei-zure	con-fu-sion	su-per-vi-sion
trea-sure	con-ver-sion	te-le-vi-sion
ver-sion	co-rro-sion	un-u-su-al
vi-sion	de-ci-sion	u-su-a-lly
	di-vi-sion	vi-su-a-lize
	en-clo-sure	
	e-ro-sion	
	ex-plo-sion	
	in-clu-sion	
	mea-sure-ment	
	tre-a-su-ry	
	vi-su-al	

<u>**Final zh by Syllables**</u>

2 Syllables	**3 Syllables**
co-lage	Ba-ton Rouge
cor-sage	bon vo-yage
ga-rage	ca-mou-flage
ma-ssage	con-ci-erge
mi-rage	en-tou-rage
pre-sage	sa-bo-tage

The S Sound: Make the S by lightly placing your tongue near the top of your mouth on the ridge behind your front teeth. The air should pass over the top of the tongue in an even way. The tongue is relaxed. While making the sound, do not press or tense the tongue–let it naturally lower slightly as air passes over. Sometimes people develop a whistle or slight lisp on S because the tongue is not even.

Everyone's mouth is different, and the position of your teeth can also affect your S sound by forcing your tongue to be off center. You may have to practise until you find the position that works for you.

The S sound is all about the free flow of air over the tongue. Record yourself and listen to see if the sound seems blocked. This can mean that your tongue is too tense, that it's pushing up on the top of your mouth (which stops the air) or that it is touching your front teeth. The tongue should be in a relaxed, neutral position toward the top of the mouth.

sack	serve	system	solar	spring	accept
sad	set	sit	soil	spree	access
saddle	six	school	soldier	sprain	process
safe	simple	sketch	soy	street	procedures
sail	silver	skill	song	stay	stations
salt	sincere	so	soothe	star	stains
sand	single	soft	soon	cent	smells
same	sink	some	soup	city	senses
sell	sister	sofa	suit	success	sleeps

Chapter 4-VOCABULARY

SYNONYMS FOR EVERYDAY WORDS

Anger - Infuriate

Answer - reply, retort-answer

Awful - dreadful, terrible, abominable, bad, poor, unpleasant

Bad - evil, immoral, wicked, corrupt, sinful, depraved, rotten, contaminated, spoiled, tainted, harmful, injurious, unfavorable, defective, inferior, imperfect, substandard, faulty, improper, inappropriate, unsuitable, disagreeable, unpleasant, cross, nasty, unfriendly, irascible, horrible, atrocious, outrageous, scandalous, infamous, wrong, noxious, sinister, putrid, snide, deplorable, dismal, gross, heinous, nefarious, base, obnoxious, detestable, despicable, contemptible, foul, rank, ghastly, execrable

Beautiful - pretty, lovely, handsome, attractive, gorgeous, dazzling, splendid, magnificent, comely, fair, ravishing, graceful, elegant, fine, exquisite, aesthetic, pleasing, shapely, delicate, stunning, glorious, heavenly, resplendent, radiant, glowing, blooming, sparkling

Begin - start, open, launch, initiate, commence, inaugurate, originate

Big - enormous, huge, immense, gigantic, vast, colossal, gargantuan, large, sizable, grand, great, tall, substantial, mammoth, astronomical, ample, broad, expansive, spacious, stout, tremendous, titanic, mountainous

Brave - courageous, fearless, dauntless, intrepid, plucky, daring, heroic, valorous, audacious, bold, gallant, valiant, doughty, mettlesome

Break - fracture, rupture, shatter, smash, wreck, crash, demolish, atomize

Bright - shining, shiny, gleaming, brilliant, sparkling, shimmering, radiant, vivid, colourful, lustrous, luminous, incandescent, intelligent, knowing, quick-witted, smart, intellectual

Calm - quiet, peaceful, still, tranquil, mild, serene, smooth, composed, collected, unruffled, level-headed, unexcited, detached, aloof

Come - approach, advance, near, arrive, reach

Cool - chilly, cold, frosty, wintry, icy, frigid

Crooked - bent, twisted, curved, hooked, zigzag

Cry - shout, yell, yowl, scream, roar, bellow, weep, wail, sob, bawl

Cut - gash, slash, prick, nick, sever, slice, carve, cleave, slit, chop, crop, lop, reduce

Dangerous - perilous, hazardous, risky, uncertain, unsafe

Dark - shadowy, unlit, murky, gloomy, dim, dusky, shaded, sunless, black, dismal, sad

Decide - determine, settle, choose, resolve

Definite - certain, sure, positive, determined, clear, distinct, obvious

Delicious - savory, delectable, appetizing, luscious, scrumptious, palatable, delightful, enjoyable, toothsome, exquisite

Describe - portray, characterize, picture, narrate, relate, recount, represent, report, record

Destroy - ruin, demolish, raze, waste, kill, slay, end, extinguish

Difference - disagreement, inequity, contrast, dissimilarity, incompatibility

Do - execute, enact, carry out, finish, conclude, effect, accomplish, achieve, attain

Dull - boring, tiring, tiresome, uninteresting, slow, dumb, stupid, unimaginative, lifeless, dead, insensible, tedious, wearisome, listless, expressionless, plain, monotonous, humdrum, dreary

Eager - keen, fervent, enthusiastic, involved, interested, alive to

End - stop, finish, terminate, conclude, close, halt, cessation, discontinuance

Enjoy - appreciate, delight in, be pleased, indulge in, luxuriate in, bask in, relish, devour, savor, like

Explain - elaborate, clarify, define, interpret, justify, account for

Fair - just, impartial, unbiased, objective, unprejudiced, honest

Fall - drop, descend, plunge, topple, tumble

False - fake, fraudulent, counterfeit, spurious, untrue, unfounded, erroneous, deceptive, groundless, fallacious

Famous - well-known, renowned, celebrated, famed, eminent, illustrious, distinguished, noted, notorious

Fast - quick, rapid, speedy, fleet, hasty, snappy, mercurial, swiftly, rapidly, quickly, snappily, speedily, lickety-split, posthaste, hastily, expeditiously, like a flash

Fat - stout, corpulent, fleshy, beefy, paunchy, plump, full, rotund, tubby, pudgy, chubby, chunky, burly, bulky, elephantine

Fear - fright, dread, terror, alarm, dismay, anxiety, scare, awe, horror, panic, apprehension

Fly - soar, hover, flit, wing, flee, waft, glide, coast, skim, sail, cruise

Funny - humorous, amusing, droll, comic, comical, laughable, silly

Get - acquire, obtain, secure, procure, gain, fetch, find, score, accumulate, win, earn, rep, catch, net, bag, derive, collect, gather, glean, pick up, accept, come by, regain, salvage

Go - recede, depart, fade, disappear, move, travel, proceed

Good - excellent, fine, superior, wonderful, marvelous, qualified, suited, suitable, apt, proper, capable, generous, kindly, friendly, gracious, obliging, pleasant, agreeable, pleasurable, satisfactory, well-behaved, obedient, honorable, reliable, trustworthy, safe, favourable, profitable, advantageous, righteous, expedient, helpful, valid, genuine, ample, salubrious, estimable, beneficial, splendid, great, noble, worthy, first-rate, top-notch, grand, sterling, superb, respectable, edifying

Great - noteworthy, worthy, distinguished, remarkable, grand, considerable, powerful, much, mighty

Gross - improper, rude, coarse, indecent, crude, vulgar, outrageous, extreme, grievous, shameful, uncouth, obscene, low

Happy - pleased, contented, satisfied, delighted, elated, joyful, cheerful, ecstatic, jubilant, gay, tickled, gratified, glad, blissful, overjoyed

Hate - despise, loathe, detest, abhor, disfavor, dislike, disapprove, abominate

Have - hold, possess, own, contain, acquire, gain, maintain, believe, bear, beget, occupy, absorb, fill, enjoy

Help - aid, assist, support, encourage, back, wait on, attend, serve, relieve, succor, benefit, befriend, abet

Hide - conceal, cover, mask, cloak, camouflage, screen, shroud, veil

Hurry - rush, run, speed, race, hasten, urge, accelerate, bustle

Hurt - damage, harm, injure, wound, distress, afflict, pain

Idea - thought, concept, conception, notion, understanding, opinion, plan, view, belief

Important - necessary, vital, critical, indispensable, valuable, essential, significant, primary, principal, considerable, famous, distinguished, notable, well-known

Interesting - fascinating, engaging, sharp, keen, bright, intelligent, animated, spirited, attractive, inviting, intriguing, provocative, though-provoking, challenging, inspiring, involving, moving, titillating, tantalizing, exciting, entertaining, piquant, lively, racy, spicy, engrossing, absorbing, consuming, gripping, arresting, enthralling, spellbinding, curious, captivating, enchanting, bewitching, appealing

Keep - hold, retain, withhold, preserve, maintain, sustain, support

Kill - slay, execute, assassinate, murder, destroy, cancel, abolish

Lazy - indolent, slothful, idle, inactive, sluggish

Little - tiny, small, diminutive, shrimp, runt, miniature, puny, exiguous, dinky, cramped, limited, itsy-bitsy, microscopic, slight, petite, minute

Look - gaze, see, glance, watch, survey, study, seek, search for, peek, peep, glimpse, stare, contemplate, examine, gape, ogle, scrutinize, inspect, leer, behold, observe, view, witness, perceive, spy, sight, discover, notice, recognize, peer, eye, gawk, peruse, explore

Love - like, admire, esteem, fancy, care for, cherish, adore, treasure, worship, appreciate, savor

Make - create, originate, invent, beget, form, construct, design, fabricate, manufacture, produce, build, develop, do, effect, execute, compose, perform, accomplish, earn, gain, obtain, acquire, get

Mark - label, tag, price, ticket, impress, effect, trace, imprint, stamp, brand, sign, note, heed, notice, designate

Mischievous - prankish, playful, naughty, roguish, waggish, impish, sportive

Move - plod, go, creep, crawl, inch, poke, drag, toddle, shuffle, trot, dawdle, walk, traipse, mosey, jog, plug, trudge, slump, lumber, trail, lag, run, sprint, trip, bound, hotfoot, high-tail, streak, stride, tear, breeze, whisk, rush, dash, dart, bolt, fling, scamper, scurry, skedaddle, scoot, scuttle, scramble, race, chase, hasten, hurry, hump, gallop, lope, accelerate, stir, budge, travel, wander, roam, journey, trek, ride, spin, slip, glide, slide, slither, coast, flow, sail, saunter, hobble, amble, stagger, paddle, slouch, prance, straggle, meander, perambulate, waddle, wobble, pace, swagger, promenade, lunge

Moody - temperamental, changeable, short-tempered, glum, morose, sullen, mopish, irritable, testy, peevish, fretful, spiteful, sulky, touchy

Neat - clean, orderly, tidy, trim, dapper, natty, smart, elegant, well-organized, super, desirable, spruce, shipshape, well-kept, shapely

New - fresh, unique, original, unusual, novel, modern, current, recent

Old - feeble, frail, ancient, weak, aged, used, worn, dilapidated, ragged, faded, broken-down, former, old-fashioned, outmoded, passe, veteran, mature, venerable, primitive, traditional, archaic, conventional, customary, stale, musty, obsolete, extinct

Part - portion, share, piece, allotment, section, fraction, fragment

Place - space, area, spot, plot, region, location, situation, position, residence, dwelling, set, site, station, status, state

Plan - plot, scheme, design, draw, map, diagram, procedure, arrangement, intention, device, contrivance, method, way, blueprint

Popular - well-liked, approved, accepted, favorite, celebrated, common, current

Predicament - quandary, dilemma, pickle, problem, plight, spot, scrape, jam

Put - place, set, attach, establish, assign, keep, save, set aside, effect, achieve, do, build

Quiet - silent, still, soundless, mute, tranquil, peaceful, calm, restful

Right - correct, accurate, factual, true, good, just, honest, upright, lawful, moral, proper, suitable, apt, legal, fair

Run - race, speed, hurry, hasten, sprint, dash, rush, escape, elope, flee

Say/Tell - inform, notify, advise, relate, recount, narrate, explain, reveal, disclose, divulge, declare, command, order, bid, enlighten, instruct, insist, teach, train, direct, issue, remark, converse, speak, affirm, suppose, utter, negate, express, verbalize, voice, articulate, pronounce, deliver, convey, impart, assert, state, allege, mutter, mumble, whisper, sigh, exclaim, yell, sing, yelp, snarl, hiss, grunt, snort, roar, bellow, thunder, boom, scream, shriek, screech, squawk, whine, philosophize, stammer, stutter, lisp, drawl, jabber, protest, announce, swear, vow, content, assure, deny, dispute

Scared - afraid, frightened, alarmed, terrified, panicked, fearful, unnerved, insecure, timid, shy, skittish, jumpy, disquieted, worried, vexed, troubled, disturbed, horrified, terrorized, shocked, petrified, haunted, timorous, shrinking, tremulous, stupefied, paralyzed, stunned, apprehensive

Show - display, exhibit, present, note, point to, indicate, explain, reveal, prove, demonstrate, expose

Slow - unhurried, gradual, leisurely, late, behind, tedious, slack

Stop - cease, halt, stay, pause, discontinue, conclude, end, finish, quit

Story - tale, myth, legend, fable, yarn, account, narrative, chronicle, epic, sage, anecdote, record, memoir

Strange - odd, peculiar, unusual, unfamiliar, uncommon, queer, weird, outlandish, curious, unique, exclusive, irregular

Take - hold, catch, seize, grasp, win, capture, acquire, pick, choose, select, prefer, remove, steal, lift, rob, engage, bewitch, purchase, buy, retract, recall, assume, occupy, consume

Tell - disclose, reveal, show, expose, uncover, relate, narrate, inform, advise, explain, divulge, declare, command, order, bid, recount, repeat

Think - judge, deem, assume, believe, consider, contemplate, reflect, mediate

Trouble - distress, anguish, anxiety, worry, wretchedness, pain, danger, peril, disaster, grief, misfortune, difficulty, concern, pains, inconvenience, exertion, effort

True - accurate, right, proper, precise, exact, valid, genuine, real, actual, trusty, steady, loyal, dependable, sincere, staunch

Ugly - hideous, frightful, frightening, shocking, horrible, unpleasant, monstrous, terrifying, gross, grisly, ghastly, horrid, unsightly, plain, homely, evil, repulsive, repugnant, gruesome

Unhappy - miserable, uncomfortable, wretched, heart-broken, unfortunate, poor, downhearted, sorrowful, depressed, dejected, melancholy, glum, gloomy, dismal, discouraged, sad

Use - employ, utilize, exhaust, spend, expend, consume, exercise

Wrong - incorrect, inaccurate, mistaken, erroneous, improper, unsuitable

Vocabulary for Everyday use

Word List 1

1. Reject–not Like
2. Delighted–Happy
3. Slumber–Deep Sleep
4. Vigilant–Alert
5. Audacity–Persistent
6. Bestowed–gievn as a Blessing
7. Revenge–to Pay Back
8. Mock–to Make fun of
9. Startled–Shoched
10. Misuse–not use Correctly

Word List 1

1. Hunchback–Person with Bent Shoulders
2. Deceived–Cheated
3. Malicious–Harmful
4. Monotonous–Same Type
5. Captivated–Captured by Something/Someone
6. Adore–to Love
7. Corpse–Dead Body
8. Discreet–Quite Secretive

9. Delicacy–Tasty Dis
10. Bizarre–not Normal

Word List 3

1. Tactfully–with Skill
2. Restore–Bring Back
3. Inaccessible–which cannot be Reached
4. Anticipation–Hope
5. Endurance–Tolerance
6. Rampage–Running Around
7. Swayed–Moved
8. Gaped–to State Open–Mouthed
9. Leaned–Bent
10. Fade Away–Disappear

Word List 4 Frail–weak

1. Turn down–refuse
2. Wear out–become very tired
3. Wrap up–finish something
4. Cynical–crazy
5. Futile–useless
6. Awesome–good
7. Awestruck–shocked
8. Rejoice–celebrate
9. Equivalent–of equal value
10. Astonishing–surprising
11. Approved–given permission for
12. Advanced–higher in level
13. Alike–same

14. Amidst–among
15. Approximate–almost near
16. Amiable–friendly
17. Avoid–not talk to someone
18. Afraid–scared
19. Adventure–interesting happening
20. Accrued–collected

WORDS TO CREATE STORIES WITH MEANINGS AND STORY EXAMPLES

The Alphabet A

1. Astonishing–surprising
2. Approved–given permission for
3. Advanced–higher in level
4. Alike–same
5. Amidst–among
6. Approximate–almost near
7. Amiable–friendly
8. Avoid–not talk to someone
9. Afraid–scared
10. Adventure–interesting happening
11. Accrued–collected
12. Altercation–fight
13. Associate–to know someone
14. Apart–leaving that thing
15. Appoint–to give a position to
16. Applied–put into effect
17. Action–something we do

18. Acclaim–to be known
19. Annoyed–angry
20. Aloof–to stay away from others

Astonishing Action

One day a man was **astonished** to find an **altercation** with complete **action** taking place on the road. He did not **approve** of such fights which people sometimes treated as **adventure**.

He went **aloof** as he did not like it amidst the crowd. He was very **annoyed** at the way people were so apart. He wanted everyone to **associate** and **avoidaltercations**. **Accrued** anger, he was **afraid** would create hatred and he **appointed** himself as a peace-maker. He **applied** his rules of peace to the world and, **approximately** at the age of 30, he became a great peace-maker and got **acclaim.**

Alphabet B

1. Boasting–talking high of oneself
2. Blister–a boil
3. Blunt–not sharp
4. Boring–dull
5. Broader–bigger in width
6. Broadcast–tell loud
7. Bluffer–who speaks less
8. Blocked–stopped
9. Bridged–having a connection
10. Bossier–who bosses/rules more
11. Basement–A floor below the ground
12. Betterment–for the better of someone

13. Blamed–to complain
14. Blackout–no lights at all
15. Brunch–Meal before lunch
16. Bonfire–Fire outside for fun
17. Brainstorm–brilliant idea
18. Branded–having a good company name
19. Brightened–make brighter
20. Bouquet–flowers together

The Boasting Child

One day in a city far away there lived a child named Claudia. She was in the habit of **boasting** about things.

One morning she burnt her hand and got a **blister**.She told her friends that she had cut her hand with a knife which was not **blunt**.

Her friends she was lying and found the story **boring** and considered her a **bluffer**.

They **blamed** her for lying . After that, she got angry and ran away.The road became **broader** and she reached a**basement**.There was a **bonfire** in the basement and a **bouquet** of flowers was kept.The room was **brightened** with lights. Claudia got scared and ran away as she had seen a monster.Over**brunch** she told her friends what she had seen but no one believed her.

Alphabet C

1. Creature–A species/living things
2. Commence–to start
3. Claustrophobia–feeling of breathlessness
4. Crucial–important
5. Critical–very important

6. Conversation–talk between people
7. Comforting–assuring/making comfortable
8. Clutter–junk, dirt
9. Cloned–made like original
10. Conceited–who thinks high of himself
11. Clipped–shortened
12. Closet–cupboard
13. Culprit–person who has done wrong
14. Cropped–made short
15. Chopped–cut into small pieces
16. Compulsory–important to do
17. Cramped–less space
18. Cracked–having cracks
19. Collide–to bang with someone
20. Clumsy–a person who is careless

The Claustrophobic Creature

In a river near the mountain lived a **creature** who was **claustrophobic.**

It was **crucial** for him to **commence** the treatment for this problem.He had a **critical conversation** with his doctor who was very **comforting**. He told the creature to first remove all the **clutter** from his river house. He told him not to be **conceited** and **clone** the **cleanliness** of the fish that lived in the river.

The creature cleaned his closet and the room was less **cramped**. The cracked surface on which he **collided** was also **chopped**. He knew that he was the **culprit** who kept his room dirty. He decided not to be **clumsy** and made it **compulsory** to drop dirtiness from the room and live a happy life.

Alphabet D

1. Drastic–sudden and Impactful
2. Dramatic–doing something with extra emotions
3. Desirable–Something wished for
4. Drizzled–light rain
5. Definite–sure
6. Damp–little wet
7. Dumped–throw
8. Delightful–nice
9. Deserving–person who should get something
10. Docile–sweet and shy
11. Drapes–curtains
12. Delivery–giving something at home
13. Depth–how deep something is
14. Deadlier–more harmful
15. Dignified–graceful
16. Droopy–sleepy
17. Dizzy–fainting
18. Drowsy–sleepy
19. Depressed–sad
20. Dejected–sad and feeling unwanted

The Drastic Decision

Mia lived with her mother in England. She was very **dramatic** and there were many things which were **desirable** to her. One morning it **drizzled** outside and the weather was damp. She made a definite and **drastic** decision not to go to school. She **dumped** her bag and began thinking of **delightful** things to do. She was not docile and felt that she

deserved more in life. She drew the drapes so that no one could see her. She then had a pizza **delivered.** As she thought in **depth** she got a **deadlier** idea and she decided to put on make-up to look **dignified** like her mother.She played forhours and then felt **dizzy** and **drowsy.**This **depressed** her as she wanted to play more. Finally,**dejected** she slept off till her mother woke the next day.

Alphabet E

1. Encyclopedia–a book of important information
2. Enraged–angry
3. Ecstatic–excited
4. Eagerly–waiting with excitement
5. Enthusiasm–energy and excitement
6. Escaped–to run away without anyone knowing
7. Effort–hard work put in to do something
8. Extrovert–person who loves to interact with others
9. Excited–very happy
10. Erratic–not in a fixed order
11. Errand–some task to do
12. Exclusive–only for one person/thing
13. Episode–part of something
14. Exclude–leave from something
15. Entered–to get inside a room
16. Eatery–place to eat
17. Epic–long drama of ancient time
18. Enlightened–to inform/bring to light
19. Elite–high in status
20. Entrapped–trapped by someone/something

The Enraged Mother

Once in France, lived Bruno with his mother. Bruno was **ecstatic** about reading the new **encyclopedia** his mom had bought. He **eagerly** waited for her to go so that he could read it. His mother warned him not to spoil it. As she left, Bruno's **enthusiasm** made him take the **effort** of opening the book to read. His **extrovert** nature brought **erratic** thoughts to his mind. He decided to keep the book **exclusively** for himself and **entered** the living room with his thoughts.He did not want to **exclude** his friend Sam from the **excitement.** He called him for an **errand** at the **eatery**. Both of them got busy in the book and suddenly the parcel of pastries fell on it. Bruno's mother was **enraged** and punished both the boys but later was **enlightened** about how it happened and she forgave them.

Alphabet F

1. Frozen–hardened because of cold
2. Frustrated–angry
3. Frightened–scared
4. Frothy–with foam/soapy
5. Frankly–honestly
6. Freaky–scary
7. Failure–not successful
8. Fumble–not able to talk clearly
9. Flaps–opening
10. Flopped–lose
11. Flowing–moving like water
12. Feverish–having a feeling of fever
13. Former–the previous one
14. Flamboyantly–at a large scale

15. Flames–fire sparks
16. Flakey–snow like pieces
17. Frequently–often
18. Fortune–lot of money/good luck

The Frozen City

Once upon a time near the north pole was a city which had **frozen** because of the cold. The people were **frustrated** and **frightened**. Roads had become **frothy** with the water and, quite **frankly**, people were **freaky** because of their failure to change anything. The cold made people **fumble** and would keep their hands in their jacket **flaps**. Attempts to beat the winter had **flopped** and water was **flowing** everywhere. People felt **feverish** and prayed for the former weather to come back.Then one day after a large meeting the sun **flamboyantly** shone in the sky and its hot **flames** made the snow **flakey**. After that day the people of the city **frequently** prayed and were happy with that **fortune**.

Alphabet G

1. Gigantic–very large
2. Gorgeous–beautiful
3. Grumpy–angry
4. Glorified–with lot of fame
5. Gratitude–thankfulness/respect
6. Grand–nice/at a large scale
7. Gazing–seeing
8. Gauge–bandage
9. Grose–not nice
10. Gripped–hold tightly
11. Greatness–niceness

12. Grating–cutting into small pieces
13. Greedy–who is not satisfied
14. Grease–kind of oil
15. Grinning–smiling
16. Generous–who is ready to give everything
17. Glittered–shining
18. Gifted–talented
19. Gutter–drain
20. Garbage–waste things

The Gigantic Mountains

Once upon a time in a far away land there were **gigantic** mountains covered with snow. They looked so **gorgeous** that even a **grumpy** face would have a smile on seeing them. People **glorified** its beauty and thanked God with **gratitude** for having made such a **grand** delight. Tourists **gazed** at its beauty and no one found anything **gross** in it.The beauty **gripped** people's interest and they talked far and wide about its greatness. But one day a **greedy** businessman bought a part of the mountain and trucks filled with **grease** spilled on the mountain. **Generous** portions of grease fell everywhere. The **glitter** of the God-gifted mountain turned into the sight of a **gutter** or **garbage** and slowly the popularity of the mountains finished.

Alphabet H

1. Hatred–feeling of hate for someone
2. Happiness–feeling of joy
3. Hamper–a gift/spoil something
4. Honesty–truth
5. Hazard–a problem

6. Hurricane–a huge storm
7. Honour–respect
8. Hallucinate–imagining things which are not true
9. Hinder–obstruct from doing something
10. Hasty–in a hurry
11. Humble–polite
12. Hefty–broad and big
13. Hiked–increased in rate
14. Handy–useful
15. Handkerchief–a piece of cloth used to clean used to clean things
16. Hindered–stopped, obstructed
17. Hospitality–taking care of our guests
18. Handling–the way we hold something
19. Hurried–to go fast

The Hurricane

One day in a small village where people had no **hatred** for each other and there was **happiness** and **honesty** everywhere, came a big **hurricane**. It caused **hefty** damage and people **hurried** to live in other towns. Growth was **hindered** and the villagers took **hasty** decisions to sell their land.The destruction made people **hallucinate** and they lost their **humble** nature. They did not **honour** each other and their **happiness** was **hampered.**

As time passed, people realized the importance of their village and set-up a **hospitality** center for the people who, lost everything. They started **handling** life in a better way and soon the village became a happy place again.

Alphabet I

1. International–relating to all the countries

2. Introvert–who does not like to mix with people
3. Isolated–alone
4. Include–add
5. Intention–what we want to do
6. Inquisitive–curious/wanting to know things
7. Invitations–calling for a function
8. Influence–effect
9. Interaction–talking to each other
10. Innocent–not cunning
11. Inverted–tilted
12. Internally–from inside
13. Interesting–not boring
14. Immense–a lot
15. Inner–from inside
16. Imitated–copied

The Isolated Introvert

In an **international** level city lived an **introvert** named Mark who liked to stay **isolated**. He would not include anyone in his life and his **intention** to stay alone was clear. He would hate **inquisitive** people and no one gave him **invitations** to their parties. When he was very small, he came under the **influence** of bad things and his **interaction** with other had people stopped. He was **innocent** and so **inverted** that thoughts came **internally** to his mind. Nothing was more **interesting** for him and with full **intention** he became an **introvert**. One day a friend of his childhood came and understood his **immense** problems. He helped him clear his **inner** thoughts and **imitated** a doctor to make him free of his **introvertness**. Mark soon became fine and lived happily.

Alphabet J

1. Jealous–feel angry or compare with someone
2. Journey–trip
3. Jubilant–excited
4. Jovial–happy and cheerful
5. Justify–do the right thing
6. Jeopardize–spoil
7. Jumbled–mixed up
8. Jay–jealous
9. Judging–thinking with a decision
10. Jittery–uncertain
11. Jumbo–big
12. Jewellery–things to wear on the body
13. Jaguar–tigerlike animal with spots
14. Junk–old, useless things
15. Jogging–running slowly
16. Jolly–happy
17. Juggling–throwing balls in the air continuously
18. Justification–giving the reason for something
19. Jacket–a coat
20. Juicy–full of juice

The Disappointing Journey

Arthur was a **jovial** man but he had one weakness. He would get **jealous** very soon.One day he was **jubiliant**as he was going on a **journey** to Singapore. He wanted to go there as his friend had gone there a few days back. He could not **justify** the reason to go and did not want to **jeopardize** his happiness. Many **jumbled** thoughts were on his mind and he did not want to be **jay** of his friend.

Arthur was **jittery** about going alone. He packed a **jumbo** sandwich and kept money to buy **jewellery** and see the **jaguar** in the forest reserve. He carried no **junk** and **jogged** to get a taxi. His **jolly** move was suddenly ruined as he hit a rock and thoughts **juggled** in his mind. He broke his head and could not go.

No **justification** was enough to make him forget the bad event and he cried for days wearing the same **jacket** he wore to the airport.

Alphabet K

1. Knight–a soldier
2. Knowing–to be aware
3. Knowledge–to know of something
4. Knob–door handle
5. Kindness–niceness
6. Knuckle–finger joint bone
7. Kaleidoscope–many colours
8. Knelt–bent down
9. Kleptomania–a person who wants to steal
10. Knock Out–make unconsious
11. Knock over–to drop/spill
12. Knot–tying a piece of string
13. Knead–to press flour for bread
14. Knapsack–a bag
15. Kiwi–a bird
16. Kimono–a Japanese garment
17. Kennel–a dog house
18. Kidnap–taken by force
19. Kernel–soft part of coconut
20. Keen–happy/interested

The Kindness of the Night

In a large **kingdom** many years ago lived a **knight** who was full of **knowledge** and **kindness**. He was brave and knew that he was strong as a **knob**. One day there was a fight in the kingdom and soldiers wore **kaleidoscopic** uniforms.

They knew that if they **knelt** in front of the other army, the king would break their **knuckles** or kill them.The knight went to the battlefield and **knocked** out many soldiers and others were **knocked** over by others.

Suddenly, the **knot** of his uniform broke and the **knapsack** he was carrying, fell. As he picked it up he saw a woman in a **kimono** alongwith a **Kiwi**. She was bleeding from injuries. He took her to a **kennel** nearby and bandaged her, but she died. From that day he was no longer **keen** on fighting and he became a priest.

Alphabet L

1. Language–words spoken in a country
2. Lumpy–not smooth
3. Loser–who has not won
4. Limping–not walking properly
5. Lethargic–lazy
6. Lame–unable to walk normally
7. Laid–back–lazy
8. Luxurious–very rich
9. Lustrous–shiny and healthy
10. Literature–written material
11. Lullaby–a soft song sung for babies
12. Lukewarm–mildly warm
13. Lucrative–profitable

14. Luscious–rich in taste and smell
15. Lounge–a place to wait
16. Loathe–hate
17. Litter–rubbish left around
18. Literacy–ability to read and write
19. Linger–to delay
20. Limousine–a large car

The Loser

In a village lived Ram who was fourteen years old. He hated studying and was bad in every **language**. One day while walking home he ate something **lumpy** and fainted. When he woke up, he was feeling **lethargic** and **lame** as he could not walk. His **laid-back** attitude made him sit down and relax.

He started dreaming of a **luxurious** place with **lustrous** walls.He remembered kings from literature and queens singing **lullabies**. His feet was dipped in lukewarm rose water. **Luscious** cherries were in his mouth and he sat in a **lounge**. He was the owner of a **limousine** and there was no **loathe** around him.The dream **lingered** on till suddenly a bad smell woke him up and he realized he was sitting on a pile of **litter**. He ran home and washed himself and promised himself not to daydream again.

Alphabet M

1. Mandatory–compulsory to do
2. Melodramatic–behaving with emotions/dramatic
3. Meek–scared
4. Murkier–dirtier
5. Monotype–same type
6. Musical–song–like

7. Melodious–nice to hear
8. Mighty–strong
9. Mushy–shy
10. Mistaken–by error
11. Monotonous–same type
12. Mysterious–secretive
13. Magical–like magic
14. Mischief–some naughtiness
15. Magnificent–very big and beautiful
16. Massive–huge/very big
17. Monopoly–rule of one person
18. Muslin–type of cloth/material

The Musical Concert

Everyone was excited in college because it was **mandatory** to audition for the school concert. Some students were **melodramatic** during the audition and others were **meek**. Some **monotype** and **monotonous** voices were rejected. A few students with **melodious** voices, which were **magical**, passed the audition. One boy who was to do **mopping** of the floor, saw the auditions and as he stood there **mighty** and **masculine**, he was **mistaken** by the teachers to be one of the students. As he sang, his **mysterious** and **magnificent** voice impressed everyone. When the teachers came to know that the boy was selected by mistake and there was no **mischief** or **monopoly**, they decided to make him a part of the concert. So the boy threw his **muslin** and picked up the guitar to rock on.

Alphabet N

1. Naughty–who does wrong things

2. Narrating–telling
3. Nasty–bad
4. Negative–not positive
5. Neighbour–who stays near by
6. Numerous–many
7. Numb–feeling nothing
8. Needy–who needs things/poor
9. Native–who belongs to a certain country
10. Nationality–the country we belong to
11. Nausea–feeling of vomit
12. Neglect–not pay attention to
13. Nickname–the name commonly used at home
14. Niece–daughter of your brother/sister
15. Nitty-gritty–important facts
16. Nominate–to choose someone
17. Nostalgic–remembering past moments
18. Notorious–known for bad things
19. Nuisance–something annoying
20. Namesake–person having the same name as another

Naughty Nina

Mary had a naughty **niece** Nina. She would **narrate** false tales to her aunt. Mary had a **nasty neighbour** who Nina did not like. There were **numerous negative** reasons for hating this person.Nina was playing outside and the **notorious** neighbour started teasing her with her **nickname** and called her a **nuisance**. *First,* Nina **neglected** him but then she became angry. She went towards the fence and acted as if she had **nausea** and was going to vomit. The neighbour became **numb** and asked her to leave. She refused saying that she knew his **namesake** and this made her **nostalgic** so she wanted to **nominate** him as a very nice person. However, her nausea stopped her from getting into the **nitty-gritty**. The neighbour ran inside as he did not want to see her vomit and Nina, happy now, continued to play in peace.

Alphabet O

1. Optimistic–Positive minded
2. Opportunity–chance
3. Oscillated–to move from one place to another
4. Ownership–person who owns something
5. Orchard–fruit garden
6. Obstruction–stoppage/blockage
7. Offending–making a person feel bad
8. Opposing–going against something
9. Opposite–the reverse
10. Orchestra–band
11. Obsolete–which is of no use
12. Obtain–get
13. Obsession–passion for something
14. Obvious–definite
15. Occupation–profession
16. Obstinate–stubborn
17. Occassional–once in a while

The Optimistic Boy

Jack lived in a very small town but was very **optimistic** that one day he would become rich. One day an **opportunity** came his way and he **oscillated** with happiness. A man came to his house and **offered him ownership** of an **orchard** at a small price. Jack did not have the money, but he was ready to **overcome** any **obstruction**. He decided to work hard and collect the money. People discouraged him and made **offending** statements **opposing** his decision. However, Jack thought **opposite**, he joined an **orchestra** and sold **obsolete** things to collect money. Slowly, he was able to **obtain** the money and his **obsession** made him the **owner** of the **orchard**. It was **obvious** that he would work hard to take his **occupation** ahead and slowly became rich, His **obstinate** nature did not let **occasional** troubles block his path and he soon became a wealthy man.

Alphabet P

1. Pessimistic–who thinks negative
2. Pricey–showing off
3. Possession–what we have
4. Petrified–scared
5. Pampered–spoilt
6. Praising–talking good of someone
7. Plight–bad state
8. Prank–trick
9. Prompt–on time
10. Painful–pain–causing
11. Plump–fat
12. Plucked–to pick from the stem
13. Pending–waiting to finish
14. Prickly–not smooth
15. Promised–to commit something
16. Possibility–chance

17. Pleased–happy
18. Pastures–green land
19. Pauper–poor person
20. Poverty–state of being poor

The Pessimistic Lion

In a jungle near Africa, lived a lion. He was a very good king of the jungle but his **pricey** nature was his weakest **possession**. He also **petrified** other animals with his **pessimistic** nature. Even though other animals **praised** and **pampered** him, they could not change him. One day the animals decided to play a **prank** on him. They waited for him to get into his **pessimistic** mood and then the whole jungle hid from him. He was alone in his **plight** and was worried about his food which was always **promptly** delivered to him. It was painful to even think that his meal was **pending**. He was **promised** food in an hour and no one had got it. He thought of every **possibility** but could not figure it out. As time went by, he realized that life was very comfortable and he was **pleased** with it. There was no **poverty** or **paupers** and everywhere were green **pastures**. He decided that he should remain happy and changed. The animals seeing him smiling came out from hiding and lived happily ever after.

Alphabet Q

1. Quest–A mission we go to
2. Quantity–amount
3. Quizzed–asked questions
4. Quarrel–fight
5. Quit–to leave
6. Quiver–to shake,tremble

7. Quieten–to make silent
8. Quilt–a bed cover
9. Queue–a line
10. Queer–strange
11. Queasy–feeling vomitish
12. Qualify–to pass a test
13. Quibble–to argue
14. Quicksand–loose wet sand that can suck in people
15. Quickly–fast
16. Quench–to satisfy, extinguish
17. Questionnaire–a list of questions to be answered
18. Quality–degree of excellence
19. Quake–to shake

The Quset

Mark was chosen by the adventure club to go on a **quest**. He was **quizzed** to know his comfort and though many quarrelled to take his position, Mark was not ready to **quit**. The quest was a big one and people **quivered** at the thought of taking it alone. Mark set out for his destination, **quietened** by the lonely roads. At night he slept under his **quilt** which was **queer** for him. He felt **queasy** at times but wanted to **quench** his thirst for adventure. As he moved on, he saw a **queue** in front. Someone had fallen into **quicksand** after a **quibble**. People were **questioning** each other to **qualify** someone for the rescue. Mark, immediately jumped to save the man. The earth **quaked** under his weight but he quickly pulled the man out. The man thanked him and wanted to reward him. He gave him his blessings and a lot of money which helped Mark complete his quest, though in his heart he knew that his true **quest** was saving the man.

Alphabet R

1. Renovate–to make changes
2. Rusting–getting spoiled
3. Rampage–to rush around
4. Referred–to give reference to
5. Rustic–village-like
6. Righteous–honest
7. Rectify–correct
8. Reserved–kept for someone
9. Reliable–one we can depend on
10. Reasoning–finding the reasons
11. Rapidly–very fast
12. Rendezvous–meeting place
13. Rifted–shifted/moved
14. Rowdy–rough behaviour
15. Racist–one who talks of caste
16. Rubble–broken bricks
17. Routine–what we do every day
18. Resuming–starting again
19. Rumour–gossip/false story
20. Revive–bring to life again

The House Renovation

Peter had a beautiful house near the country side. However, its certain parts were **rusting**and he wanted to **rectify** them. He went on a **rampage** to get the house **renovated**. A friend **referred** him to an architect who was ready to change the **rustic** look of his house. Peter found him **reliable** and after **reasoning** out things over a

rendezvous,the **renovation** started **rapidly**. *First* the **rubbles** were **repaired** and **rifted** blocks were put back. **Routine** checking was done and the beauty of the house started to **revive**. One day a **rowdy** group of the village who were **racists** came to break Peter's house, because they were jealous of him. This **rumour** had reached Peter and he put an electric fence around the house. The **rowdy** boys got electrocuted and work on the house was **resumed.**

Alphabet S

1. Sincere–commited and honest
2. Significant–important
3. Surprised–shocked
4. Solidify–make strong
5. Strength–energy
6. Strenuous–difficult to do
7. Sly–wicked
8. Scenario scene
9. Seeping–leaking in
10. Scenic–from a scene
11. Strain–difficult
12. Stuck–which cannot come out of a situation
13. Satisfaction–content and happy
14. Sluggish–lazy
15. Sleek–sharp and good-looking
16. Separate–not together
17. Stepped–put foot on someone/something
18. Stony–stonelike
19. Suffocated–not able to breath
20. Significance–importance

Sincere Sam

Sam was a nine year old **sincere** boy. There was nothing **significant** in him but he surprised everyone with his mental **strength**. He could **solidify** his mind and do **strenuous** studying. He never thought of **sly** things and would not let bad thoughts **seep** into his mind. One night before a difficult exam, the **scenario** changed. Even though he tried and **strained** his mind, he could not remember his notes. His learning was not to his **satisfaction**. He felt **sluggish** and nothing seemed **sleek**. He felt that his room was **suffocating** which could be a **significant** cause. He **stepped** out of the house and took breaths of fresh air which made him separate from his **sluggishness** and he was fresh again.

Alphabet T

1. Temper–anger
2. Troubled–having a problem
3. Tasty–good to eat
4. Trust–having faith
5. Terrible–very bad
6. Terrified–scared
7. Tolerable–which you can bear
8. Tenure–time period
9. Triggered–started
10. Trapped–cannot come out
11. Tolerant–one who is patient and does not get angry
12. Torn–to pull apart
13. Tough–not easy to destroy
14. Tampered–touched or spoilt
15. Tricked–cheated

16. Tracked–found location
17. Tickling–making someone laugh
18. Trickling–falling slowly like liquid
19. Tease–to make fun of
20. Technique–a method of doing something

The Tasty Cake

A little boy lived in a small house in the city. His mother lost her **temper** on him as she was **troubled** by his naughty behaviour. She **trusted** him with some work which he did a **terrible** job of. Her **tenure** at office was also coming to an end and she was **terrified** of losing her job. She was **tolerant** of him but had become **tough** lately. As his mother left for office an idea **triggered** the boy's mind and he he decided to bake a cake for his mom to make her happy. He wore clean clothes and tried looking for the **technique** to bake a cake. He **tracked** down a book but some pages were **torn** and **tampered**. The recipe of the plum cake **tricked** him but he continued it. Thecake was easy to make but the icing **trickled** down the cake. It was ready by the time his mom came home. She was surprised and he **teased** and **tickled** her to make her laugh. She was taken aback and was **trapped** in his love for ever.

Alphabet U

1. Undisputed–which cannot be questioned
2. Undertake–to agree to a task
3. Undesirable–not wanted
4. Under-priviliged–those who are poor
5. Unhappy–sad
6. Undone–spoiled
7. Unreasonable–not sensible

8. Unreal–imaginary
9. Unpleasant–not nice
10. Unscrew–to take the screws out
11. Unseen–not seen
12. Unstable–not fixed properly
13. Untried–not tried
14. Untidy–not clean
15. Unthinkable–which is not expected to happen
16. Unused–not used
17. Untrue–false
18. Unwell–not well
19. Unusual–strange
20. Unvoiced–not told about

The Under-Priviliged Village

Near a city was a village where people lived in an **undisputed** and bad condition. They **undertook** small jobs and were very **unhappy**. Their **unreasonable** and **unpleasant** living conditions were **unseen** by the governing body. Their life was **unthinkable** and **unstable**. One day a man of the village was **unwell** and he had a farm which was **unused** alongwith a tractor. He called the villagers and told them that a pot of gold was hidden in his farm, but only that person could get it who would go through **unusual** and **untried** situations. The villagers needed the money as their demands were **unvoiced**. They had to open a large door, so they began to **unscrew** the lock. They took the tractor and ploughed the field but there was nothing. They put seeds on it as instructed by the man, but nothing was found. A few days later the crop came and the villagers were able to sell it. They realized that this was the gold the man had talked about.

Alphabet V

1. Victory–to win
2. Victorious–a person who wins
3. Violent–not peaceful
4. Vicious–cruel
5. Versatile–having a lot of qualities
6. Vigour–energy
7. Volatile–having a lot of power
8. Veterinary–branch of medicine dealing with animals
9. Visible–which can be seen
10. Victim–who gets harmed
11. Vicinity–locality
12. Ventilation–allowing fresh air
13. Vendor–a person who sells things
14. Venom–poisonous fluid
15. Vanquish–to destroy
16. Vanity–conceit
17. Vanished–disappeared
18. Vary–to be different
19. Valuable–important

The Victorious Vendor

Once upon a time there was a **versatile vendor** who was **victorious** in whatever he did. However, he was envied by everyone in the **vicinity**. People wanted to **vanquish** him. The vendor's **vigour** made him **vanish** his thoughts of **vanity**. One day another vendor decided to steal his **valuable** things and put **venom** in his tea. The evil **vendor** went to the good vendor and asked for some **velvet**. As he left to get the **velvet, viscious** thoughts made the evil person put venom in the tea. When the good vendor came back. he saw that the man had **vanished** and was not **visible** anymore. He started having his tea but remembered that he had to deliver the goods. As he got up, the tea fell and a dog drank it and died. Seeing the dog die, he learnt his **valuable** lesson, not to trust anyone blindly.

Alphabet W

1. Wailing–crying
2. Wagging–moving from one place to another
3. Wandering–moving without purpose
4. Walk away–to leave
5. Waltz–a kind of dance
6. Wardrobe–cupboard
7. Welfare–is someone's happiness
8. Weird–strange
9. Wept–cried
10. Well-built–made nicely
11. Well-chosen–selected well
12. Whimper–cry
13. Whine–high pitched sound like a dog crying
14. Wheeze–not able to breathe
15. Witty–smart
16. Wobble–moving unsteadily
17. Workaholic–who loves to work
18. Worrisome–cause of worry
19. Worldwide–throughout the world
20. Worn-out–become very old

The Wailing Dog

Bosco was a friendly dog always **wagging** its tail to passers-by. One day as he was **wandering** near the walkway, a **weird** object hurt his leg. He **whimpered** and **whined** but no one came to his help. Suddenly, a **well-built** man who was returning from his **Waltz** class saw Bosco. He could not **walk-away** leaving the **wheezing** dog. He took him to a doctor who was a **workaholic** and was known **worldwide**. Bosco was **wobbling** and the doctor thought that the situation was **worrisome**. The man knew that the doctor was **well-chosen** and made **witty** comments to lighten the mood. An hour passed but the doctor was unable to cure the **wound** so he gave an injection to Bosco. Bosco was grateful to the man who became so fond of him that he took him home and they lived happily together.

Alphabet X

1. XYLOPHONE–a musical instrument
2. X–RAY–a medical process
3. X–MAS–short form of Christmas
4. XEROX–duplicate/copy

The X–Mas Party

Tina decided to have an **X-mas** party at her home. She called all her friends and **xeroxed** the invitations to send them.Her best-friend Lucy had to visit the doctor for an **X-ray** report, so she refused. She called all her friends but everyone had plans. So, poor Tina had to celebrate X-mas alone with her **xylophone**, eating the cake and singing Christmas carols.

Alphabet Y

1. Yawning–opening mouth when sleeping
2. Yelling–shouting
3. Yearn–want badly
4. Yank–pull hard

5. Yummy–tasty
6. Youth–young
7. Yolk–yellow of an egg
8. Yucky–bad
9. Yesterday–the day before
10. Yoghurt–thick curd
11. Yo-Yo–kind of toy
12. Yacht–a ship
13. Yam–kind of sweet potato
14. Yak–mountain animal
15. Yodel–changing sounds while sleeping
16. Yield–produce
17. Yards–a measure of distance
18. Youthful–feeling of being young
19. Youngster–young person
20. Yeast–substance used to make bread

The Yucky Yoghurt

Nina woke up **yawning**, only to find her mother **yelling** at her to hurry up. She **yearned** for a holiday and **yanked** at her mother's arm to let her go back to sleep. Her mother told her that if she would go to school she would give her some **yummy yoghurt** for dinner and a trip on a **yacht** during her holidays. Nina went to school and the **youngster** waited for her yoghurt. She played with her **yo-yo** and ate some **yam** as she waited for her mother to return with the yoghurt. Her wait **yielded** positive results and her mom was back with the same, but it tasted **yucky** because excess **yeast** had been used. Her mother asked her to bring some more from the shop which was two **yards** away. The**youthful** teenager set out **yodelling** away and patting the **yak** on the field. She bought two different flavours and ate them on her way home.

Alphabet Z

1. Zig-Zag–not straight
2. Zeal–energy
3. Zillion–an indefinite number
4. Zodiac–birth signs
5. Zoom–to go at a high speed
6. Zenith–the highest point
7. Zone–area
8. Zebra–an animal
9. Zoo–a place where animals are kept

The Zebra Crossing

In a city with many **zig-zag** roads lived a boy who would believe a lot in **Zodiacs**. One day his zodiac read that he should not go to the west **zone**. This worried him as he had to go to the **zoo** which was on the west. His **zeal** to visit the zoo made him take the risk. His fear was at its **zenith** but he **zoomed** through the roads crossing a **zillion** feelings of fear. He remembered that his mother had asked him to have faith in himself and not zodiacs. He reached the zoo and had a great day. On returning home he decided not to believe on zodiacs only and trust God.

Chapter 5-SPEECH EXAMPLES ON DIFFERENT TOPICS

TOPIC 1: PERSEVERANCE

Challenges are things that are impossible to avoid. It's a part of life that humans try to escape from or go through. Challenges can be learning to ride a bike, studying for hours to face the test the next day and perhaps writing his speech in less than 30 minutes. Everyone has goals he has set for himself. Question is, are you willing to work hard and overcome all the problems you face in order to achieve your goal?

For athletes, a challenge they face constantly is the physical pain they endure during training and competitions. That pain is what athletes are willing to risk in order to become the best. The Famous cyclist Lance Armstrong once said, "Pain is temporary. It may last a minute, or an hour, or a day, or a year, but, eventually it will subside and something else will take its place. If I quit, however, it lasts for ever." What Armstrong says is true. Most pains will eventually heal as time passes by. But knowing that you've given up on something important can last for ever. Perseverance means to endure the pain that comes with the challenge and getting through it to become stronger.

Another way of understanding perseverance is by evaluating a challenge and finding a solution. Perseverance doesn't mean to go through a challenge and simply accept what's inflicted onto you. It is also a way to fight back to find a solution. Well-known basketball star Michael Jordan once said, "If you run into a wall, don't turn around and give up.

Figure out how to climb, go through it, or work around it." As simple as it sounds, not all challenges come up with simple solutions. Challenges aren't made easy. Persevering means to get tough, put your thinking caps on and look at the challenge at a new perspective.

Perseverance means a steady effort to maintain a course of action, belief, or purpose in spite of difficulty. In order to persevere, pain and a lot of hard thinking will be needed. Athletes are the best examples of people who persevere to become the best of the best. The key to reach your goal is to persevere.

TOPIC 2: COURAGE

A person possesses two types of courage, physical and mental. Physical courage encourages the man to do works of risk like rocket manufacturing, launching satellites, etc.

It encourages man to discover the other planets of the universe and all types of laborious works.

Moral or mental courage is found in man only. It enables man to select right or wrong and to act according to his will.

Moral courage is a rare virtue. By the help of moral courage a man selects the right path, may it be opposite to public opinion. He may have to face many troubles for the right path he has selected.

In comparison to physical courage, moral courage is far superior. A man with moral courage always does right under all circumstances. For the development of society, he may have to face criticism and opposition but he never bows to it.

Jesus Christ had rare moral courage. He taught people to lead the path of truth to achieve their goal of life, but he had to face a tough opposition from the persons who were losing their strength due to his sermons.

They conspired and the son of God was crucified. But he never left the right path which he had selected.

Prophets, saints and social reformers were the targets of attacks and fury of the world for having told the people the truth. These great persons were the men of great courage.

India also had men who had great moral courage. Mahatma Gandhi stood against the all mighty British empire for its anti Indian policies.

Subhash Chandra Bose, Lala Lajpat Rai, Chandra Shekhar Azad, Bhagat Singh, Rajguru, Sukhdeo and Asfaq-ullah-Khan were a few of the great martyrs who laid their lives for the independence of their motherland and never bowed before the British empire.

So it is rightly said that a man who has no moral courage is like an animal.

Corruption

Now-a-days corruption can be seen everywhere. It is like cancer in public life, which has not become so rampant and perpetual overnight, but in course of time. A country where leaders like Mahatma Gandhi, Sardar Patel, Lal Bahadur Shastri and Kamraj have taken birth and led a value-based society, is now facing the great problem of corruption.

When we talk of corruption in public life, it covers corruption in politics, State Government, Central Governments, "business, industry and so on. Public-dealing counters in most government offices are the places where corruption is most evident. If anybody does not pay for the work it is sure that the work won't be done.

People have grown an insatiable appetite for money in them and they can go to any extent to get money. Undoubtedly, they talk of morality and the importance of value-based life, but that is for outer show. Their inner voice says something else.

It is always crying for money. It has been seen that the officers who are deputed to look into the matters of corruption, turn out to be corrupt themselves. Our leaders, too, are not less corrupt. Thus, the network of corruption is spread all over and remains undeterred.

Corruption is seen even in the recruitment departments where appointments are ensured through reliable middle agencies. The nexus between politicians and bureaucrats works in a very sophisticated manner. Such nexus does also exist between criminals and police.

Everybody knows that criminals have no morals, hence, nothing good can we expect from them. But police are supposed to be the symbol of law and order, and discipline. Even they are indulged in corruption. This is more so because they enjoy unlimited powers and there is no action against them even on complaints and there is sufficient proof of abuse of office and high'handedness.

Corruption can be need-based or greed-based. Better governance can at least help to check the need-based corruption. Better governance can check greed-based corruption also, because punishment to the corrupt is very effective in a better-governed country.

Steps should be taken to correct the overall situation. Declarations of property and assets of the government employees should be made compulsory and routine and surprise inspections as well as raids be conducted at certain intervals.

Though it is may be very difficult to control corruption, but it is not impossible. It is not only the responsibility of the Government but ours too. We can eliminate corruption if there is a joint effort. We must have high principles to follow so that we may be models for the coming generations. Let us take the view that we will create an atmosphere free from corruption. That will be our highest achievement as human beings.

Environment

Environment means our surroundings. Land, water, air, plants, animals, solid wastes and other things that are all around us, constitute our environment. Man and environment are closely intertwined with each other and maintain a balance or equilibrium in nature.

Different groups of people working in different areas express it in various ways. When physical scientists talk about environment they generally refer to the physical environment that comprises the three inter-locking systems : The Atmosphere, the Hydrosphere and the Lithosphere.

Biologists often refer to biological environment consisting of all living organisms of the Biosphere. Similarly, social scientists refer to the social, cultural, economic and organizational environment.

Hence, environment may be defined as "the sum total of all social, cultural, economical, biological, physical and chemical factors surrounding the 'man' to give necessary protection to him."

Two types of environment we may come across. One is the natural environment of the air, water, solid waste, noise, radiation, soil, timber, wildlife and living space, etc. The second one is the man-made environment that deals with work environment, housing, technology, aesthetics, transportation, utilities, settlement, urbanization and so on.

These environmental components are considered as our resources and are mostly exploited and utilized by the men to fulfill their basic physical needs; these can be considered as the fellow members of the global eco-system with which men establish emotional, intellectual, or and physical relationships and these provide the basis for a sense of purpose of life to them.

Thus, man is firmly placed as an important part of the global ecosystem, which depends on him as much as he himself depends on it. Hence, there is a close relationship between man and environment.

Books

Books are our never failing friends. Our worldly friends may desert us but they never will. They are our best friends, philosophers and guides. Friends are plenty when the purse is full, but fair-weather friends fall off in adversity. Books, like a true friend, stand by us through thick and thin. They uphold and encourage us when we feel sad and despondent.

They lift the poor out of poverty and the wretched out of misery. They make the burden-bearer forget his burden, the sick his sufferings and the downtrodden his degradation. They bring light into darkness and sunshine into shadow.

All the same we should be very judicious in the selection of books as we do in the choice of friends. The friendship of good books is the medicine of life, but there are books that could prove more dangerous than snakes and more poisonous than scorpions. The really good books sharpen our intellect, broaden our mind, enrich our experience, widen our knowledge and uplift our morals, making us better, nobler and happier in life.

Good books are the life-blood of a nation. Books like the Gita and the Mahabharta inspire us. They make us brave, daring and dauntless. Good books are the quintessence of man's experience extending over thousands of years. They are our best companions in solitude. They are a treasure house of noble thoughts which are open to us day and night.

A book like the Ramayana is undoubtedly the best of companions. It offers us all the balm we need when life has given us a rebuff and the world looks cold and uncharitable. It is a book to be digested. It is a book to be read with diligence and attention.

Gandhiji called the Gita his mother. He said, "Today the Gita is not only my Bible or my Quran, it is more than that : it is my mother. I lost my earthly mother who gave me birth long ago, but this eternal mother has completely filled her place by my side ever since. She has never changed; she has never failed me. When I am in difficulty and distress, I seek refuge in her bosom."

Once Carlyle was asked whether he would choose the dramas of Shakespeare or the kingdom of heaven if he were given a choice between the two. He at once said that he would choose the dramas of Shakespeare and spurn the kingdom of heaven. This reply of Carlyle shows the importance of good books.

Books bring enlightenment among the people and make them fond of knowledge. Like the appetite which is removed by food, man has a craving for knowledge. He is curious to know things. It provides him with mental satisfaction.

This craving for knowledge is satisfied with the reading of books. Books are our mute friends but they are not dumb. They speak in a language which is understood by the heart of man. They bring us into communion with the greatest minds of the world and of all ages.

When we read the biographies of great men, we move and associate with them; they enshrine the noble thoughts and sublime truths of all ages. They are man's most precious heritage. They provide food for the mind. They shape our character and their influence penetrates deep down the mind. They arouse us, teach us, comfort us. A good book is the precious life-blood of a master spirit.

Good books are like gold mines. The more one works as a miner, the richer one becomes. They enlighten us and widen our vision and sympathy. A mind which is not lit with knowledge is a dark cell and a home which does not have books is an unhealthy place to live in. If people are ignorant and illiterate, they will suffer from superstitions and baseless fears.

They will be narrow-minded and mean. Books are a valuable possession. They correct us when we go astray, amuse us when we are bored and give us jolly company when we feel lonely. They provide us with extra eyes to enjoy beauty and extra ears to listen to great music.

They take us to those remote places that we have not seen, those heights we can never scale and those fairy lands we can hardly imagine. A drawing room for its decoration needs well designed furniture and printed curtains, but it cannot be complete without a book-shelf. Books have ornamental value no less than material utility.

Patriotism

Patriotism is the sentiment associated with the country one lives in. Since the country is considered motherland or fatherland, it draws the respect of the people. Thus patriotism is a noble sentiment as it is based on devotion and selfless sacrifice of the people. It is the foundation that holds the structure of the nation. It is a pious sentiment and has always been adored by the people of all the nations.

All hold the patriots of their nations in high esteem. They build either their statues or memorials on which they offer wreaths with a heavy heart.

A man who doesn't have this noble sentiment lacks the sense of self-respec, too. He is the weak end of the nation who can succumb to pressure and may not become slave himself alone, but may assist the aggressor in making the whole nation slave.

India has been prone to foreign attacks for centuries. It is neither just a chance nor a sheer miracle that the country has maintained old traditions and culture. During different periods there have been patriots who sacrificed all they had to save the motherland from the foreigners.

Right from the invasion of Babar we have Rana Sanga and Maharana Pratap during the expansionist phase of Akbar. The terror of Aurangzeb was faced by the Maratha and Punjabi patriots who gave Shivaji and Guru Govind Singh. The latter sacrificed all his four sons at the altar of the nation. Then comes Banda Bairagi who smiled when his son was dashed to pieces on a stone. His skin was cut and chilli powder sprinkled all over. The spirit remained undaunted. It was this patriotism that sustained the nation and kept the culture intact, of which we are proud.

The survival and revival of patriotism in India during British regime is just yesterday's history. This period gave India the largest number of conscientious martyrs and patriots. Right from the martyrdom of Adivasi patriot Tilka Manjhi in Bihar in 1747 the stream flew to Karnataka where Rani Chenamma of Kittur and her five associates–Rayanna, Jagvir, Nagarkatti, Chennavasappa and Balanna– laid their lives for the cause of the nation in 1824. It was from Karnataka that the anguish blew to Maharashtra and then to the North when in 1857 the whole country followed the lead of Mangal Pande, Nana Saheb, Tatya Tope and Rani Laxmibai of Jhansi.

The first war of independence took a toll of very large number of patriots in the history of India's fight for freedom. Right up to 23rd March, 1931–when Bhagat Singh, Sukhdev and Rajguru were hanged in Lahore Jail, it was a period of upsurge of patriotism that took a violent shape–was rather based on violence. It was the age of intellectual patriots which was followed by Netaji Subhash and his Azad Hind Army.

Gandhi's non-violent movement, too, produced a large number of patriots from 1921 to 1940, who sacrificed their lives or were persecuted in various ways. The year 1942, again saw a rise of violent patriots. Whether violent or non-violent, the acts of the patriots against Britishers that started in the South from Kittur in the form of a people's upsurge, ended too in the South in Hyderabad in 1947, against the tyranny of the Nizam, a stooge of the Britishers.

Spearheaded by Ganapati Amrate, Sambha Kavle, Mahadevan and Keshav Shende in Umri it took a toll of more than a thousand patriots. Patriotism in India reached its climax when lakhs of people offered Satyagraha in Goa to face the bullets of the Portugese rulers. The first to fall was Jagmohan of Vijayawada in Andhra Pradesh. Hundreds of patriots from different parts of the country laid their lives to complete the picture of free Motherland.

Indian patriotism has never taken a negative attitude. Indian patriots have never been aggressors and have never disturbed the peace of the world. It cannot be linked with State nationalism of Hitler or of Mussolini or Napoleon, which took an aggressive turn and can be called narrow patriotism. It can be associated only with the sentiments of Joan of Arc of France, Abraham Lincoln of USA and De Valera of Ireland who all had a pride for and worked for their motherland without any aggressive designs.

Culture

Culture is one of the most important and basic concepts of sociology. In sociology culture has a specific meaning. The anthropologists believe that human behaviour is called culture. In other words, the behaviour which is transmitted to us by some one is called culture.

The way of living, eating, wearing, singing, dancing and talking are all parts of a culture. In common parlance, the word culture is understood to mean beautiful, refined or interesting.

In sociology, we use the word culture to denote acquired behaviour which is shared by and transmitted among the members of the society. In other words, culture is a system of learned behaviour shared by and transmitted among the members of a social group.

Culture has been defined in various ways by sociologists and anthropologists. Following are the important definitions of culture:

E.B. Tylor defines that "Culture is that complex whole which includes knowledge, belief, art, morals, jaw, customs and any other capabilities and habits acquired by man as a member of society."

Edward Sapir says that "Culture is any socially inherited element of the life of man, material and spiritual."

Malinowski defines is thus: "Culture is the handwork of man and conventional understanding manifest in art and artifacts which persist through which he achieves his ends".

Redfield remarks that "Culture is an organised body of conventional understanding manifest in art and artifact which persisting through, characterizes a human group".

Mac Iver is of the view that "Culture is the expression of our nature in our modes of living and our thinking, intercourses in our literature, in religion, in recreation and enjoyment.

According to E.S. Bogardus "Culture is all the ways of doing and thinking of a group."

Characteristics of Culture

For a clear understanding of the concept of culture it is necessary for us to know its main characteristics. Culture has several characteristics. Following are the main characteristics of culture:

1. Culture is Learnt

Culture is not inherited biologically, but learnt socially by man. It is not an inborn tendency. There is no culture instinct as such; culture is often called learned ways of behaviour.

Unlearned behaviour such as closing the eyes while sleeping, the eye blinking reflex and so on are purely physiological; and culture shaking hands or saying namaskar or thanks and shaving and dressing, on the other hand, are culture.

Similarly, wearing clothes, combing the hair, wearing ornaments, cooking food, drinking from a glass, eating from a plate or leaf, reading a newspaper, driving a car, enacting a role in drama, singing, worship, etc., are always behaviour learnt by man culturally.

2. Cultural is Social

Culture does not exist in isolation. Neither it is an individual phenomenon. It is a product of society. It originates and develops through social interaction. It is shared by the members of society. No man can acquire culture without association with other human beings.

Man becomes man only among men. It is the culture which helps man to develop human qualities in a human environment. Deprivation is nothing but deprivation of human qualities.

3. Culture is Shared

Culture, in the sociological sense, is something shared. It is not something that an individual alone can possess. *For example,* customs, tradition, beliefs, ideas, values, morals, etc., are shared by people of a group or society.

The invention of Arya Bhatta or Albert Einstein, Charaka or Charles Darwin, the literary works of Kalidas or Keats, Dandin or Dante, the philosophical works of Confucius or Lao Tse, Shankaracharya or Swami Vivekananda, the artistic works of Ravi Verma or Raphael, etc., are all shared by a large number of people.

Culture is something adopted, used, believed, practised, or possessed by more than one person. It depends upon group life for its existence. (Robert Brerstedt)

4. Culture is Transmissive

Culture is capable of being transmitted from one generation to the next. Parents pass on culture traits to their children and they in turn to their children and so on. Culture is transmitted not through genes but by means of language. Language is the main vehicle of culture.

Language in its different forms, like reading, writing and speaking makes it possible for the present generation to understand the achievements of earlier generations.

But language itself is a part of culture. Once language is acquired, it unfolds to the individual in wide a field. Transmission of culture may take place by intuition as well as by interaction.

5. Culture is Continuous and Cumulative

Culture exists as a continuous process. In its historical growth it tends to become cumulative. Culture is growing whole, which includes in itself the achievements of the past and present and makes provision for the future achievements of mankind.

Culture may thus be conceived of as a kind of stream flowing down through the centuries from one generation to another. Hence, some sociologists like Lotion called culture the social heritage of man.

As Robert Bierstadt writes culture is the money of human race. It becomes difficult for us to imagine what society would be like without this accumulation of culture and what lives would be without it.

6. Culture is Consistent and Interconnected

Culture in its development has revealed a tendency to be consistent. At the same time different parts of culture are inter-connected.

For example, the value system of a society, is closely connected with its other aspects such as morality, religion, customs, traditions, beliefs and so on.

7. Culture is Dynamic and Adaptive

Though culture is relatively stable, it is not altogether static. It is subject to slow but constant change. Change and growth are latent in culture.

We find amazing growth in the present Indian culture when we compare it with the culture of the Vedic times. Hence, culture is dynamic.

Culture is responsive to the changing conditions of the physical world. It is adaptive. It also intervenes in the natural environment and helps man in his process of adjustment.

Just as our house shelters us from the storm, so also does our culture save us from natural dangers and assist us to survive. Few of us indeed could survive without culture.

8. Culture is Gratifying

Culture provides proper opportunities and prescribes means for the satisfaction of our needs and desires. These needs may be biological or social in nature.

Our need for food, shelter and clothing and our desire for status, name, fame and money, etc., are all, *for example*, fulfilled according to our cultural ways.

Culture determines and guides the varied activities of man. In fact, culture is defined as the process through which human beings satisfy their wants.

9. Culture Varies from Society to Society

Every society has a culture of its own. It differs from society to society. The culture of every society in unique to itself. Cultures are not uniform.

Cultural elements such as customs, traditions, morals, ideals, values, ideologies, beliefs in practices, philosophies, institutions, etc., are not uniform everywhere.

Ways of eating, speaking, greeting, dressing, entertaining, living, etc., of different sects differ significantly. Culture varies from time to time also.

No culture ever remains constant or changeless. If Manu were to come back to see the Indian society today he would be bewildered to witness the vast changes that have taken place in our culture.

10. Culture is Super Organic and Ideational

Culture is sometimes called super organic. By super organic Herbert Spencer meant that culture is neither organic nor inorganic in nature, but above these two. The term implies the social meaning of physical objectives and physiological acts.

The social meaning may be independent of physiological and physical properties and characteristics. *For example,* the social meaning of a national flag is not just a piece of coloured cloth.

The flag represents a nation. Similarly, priests and prisoners, professors and profanation, players, engineers and doctors, farmers and soldiers and others are not just biological beings. They are viewed in their society differently. Their social status and role can be understood only through culture.

Discipline

Discipline means obedience to a superior authority. Accepting the norms of the family, society, the commands of elders and obeying them is also discipline. Discipline means accepting punishment for violation. Discipline also means training of mind and character, developing self-control and the habit of obedience.

In the entire universe, there is an order and discipline. The stars, the planets, the earth on which we live, the moon and the sun we see, move according to a system of discipline. We can see that plants, insects, birds and animals too observe discipline in their lives, only man who has a thinking mind finds it difficult to observe discipline.

Discipline could be divided into two broad categories, external and internal. External discipline is that which is imposed by outside authority. It is often linked with authority and force. Discipline in the army is one such. Soldiers do not have a say in it except implicit obedience. As Tennyson says "Their's not to make reply. Their's not to reason why, their's but to do and die". A soldier in a war field cannot ask for reasons. He has to obey commands; otherwise, the war is lost.

Our ancient educational system believed in enforcing discipline by force. They used to say, if you spare the rod you will spoil the child. But that view is not correct. It will produce only negative results. That is why discipline has taken a new shape in schools and colleges now. It is call self-discipline. It is discipline by acceptance, not by imposition.

We live in a democracy. Democracy is based on the will of majority of its citizens. It has to be accepted and obeyed. Otherwise, democracy loses its meaning and leads to anarchy.

Family customs and traditions, laws of the society, and moral and spiritual laws of the religion are all to be obeyed. That is discipline. Discipline demands obedience to commands from leaders, respect for women, devotion to god, etc.

Though discipline starts at home, there is much more need for it in schools. Schools are nursing places for various virtues and values. Discipline in the classroom, on the playground and elsewhere in the school is all important. Force has no place in student discipline. Teachers are to be first disciplined, so one every who cannot control oneself, cannot control others. Students emulate teachers in way. It is more so in the matter of discipline. They observe discipline by acceptance, not by force.

Some persons argue that discipline limits freedom and that also kills the man's initiative. This is a wrong view. Indiscipline cannot bring order of growth. Self-discipline or discipline by acceptance is self-control. One controls his emotions and desires and gives room to listen to other's points of view. Man has many desires and impulses. If they are allowed free play without discipline, it will end in chaos.

Nature and society are best disciplinarians. Violate their laws, and you are in for punishment. Put your finger in fire. It burns no matter who you are. There we learn discipline by experience. That is why Gandhiji has said that discipline is learnt in adversity. It is therefore necessary that, if you wish to achieve anything enduring in life, you have to be first fall disciplined in life. Lack of discipline is like a ship without rudder.

SOME POPULAR TOPICS

SPEECH

Word limit is 150 words

1. You are Isha. You recently witnessed an abstract painting exhibition at Asra - an institution for physically challenged children. You were amazed at the creative feat of a handicapped boy who painted with his feet. Next day you decided to deliver a speech in the morning assembly on how positive thinking, encouragement and support could make even handicapped children self-reliant and confident. Write that speech in about 150 words.
2. Prepare a speech on the Harmful effects of Passive Smoking in 150 words.
3. On the occasion of Diwali you have been asked to write a speech on "Say No to Crackers" Write the speech for your school stage performance in 150 words.
4. Prepare a speech on "Health and hygiene".
5. Prepare a speech on the need for "Conservation of water and electricity".
6. Prepare a speech on "Road-safety rules".
7. Prepare a speech on "Terrorism does not stop us: life goes on under any circumstances".
8. Prepare a speech on "Terrorism a socio-political evil".

9. Prepare a speech on "Religion shakes hands with science".
10. Prepare a speech on "Corporal punishment in schools".
11. Prepare a speech on "What do children expect from teachers".
12. Prepare a speech on "Cruelty to animals".
13. Prepare a speech on "Drive safe reach safe".
14. Prepare a speech on "Spread light not poison" based on Diwali.
15. Prepare a speech on "How to get good sleep"
16. Prepare a speech on "Save water".
17. Prepare a speech on " Save Earth".
18. Prepare a speech on "Children–the future"
19. Prepare a speech on "Man vs Nature".
20. Prepare a speech on "Destruction of natural resources".
21. Prepare a speech on "Violence against women".
22. Prepare a speech on "Corruption".

ARTICLE

Word limit is 150 words

1. Write an article on " Pressure of homework".
2. Write an article on "Save wildlife".
3. Write an article on "Need of safe driving".
4. Write an article on "Need of conserving energy".
5. Write an article on "dangers of drug addiction".
6. Write an article on " How advanced technology has added to man's problems".

7. Write an article on "Menace of kidnapping".
8. Write an article on "Dietary habits leading to obesity".
9. Write an article on "Cruelty towards animals".
10. Write an article on "Ban child labour".
11. Write an article on " Limit the use of internet and computers".
12. Write an article on "Life in an Indian village".
13. Write an article on "Keep fit for good health".
14. Write an article on "The problems of parking".
15. Write an article on "Importance of Moral values".
16. Write an article on "Cellphones have made the world a small place".
17. Write an article on "Modern man a slave of luxuries".
18. Write an article on "Need-based education".
19. Write an article on "Problems faced by children".
20. Write an article on "Control yourself lest nature control you".
21. Write an article on "Need of communal harmony".
22. Write an article on "Importance of games and sports".
23. Write an article on "Media role".
24. Due to growing materialism there is a shift in the values of the youngsters. They continue pestering their parents for items like mobile phone, digital camera, car, etc., for personal use, even though there is no genuine need for the same. Write an article in not more than 150 words expressing your views on the same. Give suggestions, if any.

25. You are Kashish, a strong believer in the theory that one must eat healthy food. However, you are disturbed about the eating habits of your friend who eat a lot of junk food. Write an article for the school magazine on the problems of unhealthy eating leading to lifestyle disorders like obesity, lack of concentration, lethargy, etc. Write your article in 150 word.
26. You are shocked at the growing incidence of crime against the elderly people in the society. Most of these have been living by themselves. As a volunteer for Helpage India, write your article in 150 words focusing on how the community as a whole is responsible for looking after such people
27. The rapid increase in the number of vehicles results in traffic congestion on the roads. To add to this many public transporters violate the traffic rules. The result is chaos/confusion on the road. Write an article for the newspaper expressing your opinion on the state of traffic, failure to control/check and suggest measures to improve the situ-ation.
28. You are Geeta. You are a member of the 'Environment Club' of your school. The Secretary has asked you to write an article for the school magazine on the 'Ill-effect of deforestation'.
29. While reading the newspaper you come across the following headline 'Poaching, a Great Threat to Animal Worls.' You feel that the forest authorities should keep a strict vigil in order to prevent poaching. The local people should assist otherwise our wildlife will completely disappear and the ecological balance will be seriously disturbed. Now, write an article for a newspaper highlighting how poaching is a threat to all.

30. We human beings have created acid rain. We have so polluted our atmosphere, this acid rain is affecting everything it falls on - rivers, lakes, forests, soil, animal humans, buildings, vegetation. Awareness must be created about this among - people highlighting its causes and effects. You, therefore, decide to write an article on 'Destruction: Thy Name is Acid Rain'.
31. News channels are brimming with astrological serials. You are really bugged up to see how these channels are directing people to be superstitious. Write an article in 200 words with a suitable heading
32. In your school it came to light that some class IV staff engaged in physical abuse of children, mostly from classes 5 to 6. This incident shocks you and you decide to write an article for the school newsletter asking children to stay away from such anti-social elements. Write the article.

DEBATE

Word limit is 120 to 150 words

1. Write for or against the motion on "Today's children are very health-conscious".
2. Write for or against the motion on "Science is fact, religion is fiction".
3. Write for or against the motion on "Money and happiness are proportionate to each other".
4. Write for or against the motion on "We cannot do without advertisements".
5. Write for or against the motion on " exams should be banned".
6. Write for or against the motion on "TV channels should be limited".

7. Write for or against the motion on "Homework should be abolished".
8. Write for or against the motion on " Children should be given more freedom".
9. Write for or against the motion on "women should be put at top positions".
10. Write for or against the motion on " Books should be banned".
11. Write for or against the motion on "Internet should be banned'.
12. Write for or against the motion on "Smoking should be banned'.
13. Write for or against the motion on "Alcohol should be banned".

Chapter 6-COMMUNICATION SKILLS RECAP

Remember the following

The material of your presentation should be concise, to the point and tell an interesting story. In addition to the obvious things like content and visual aids, the following are just as important as the audience will be sub-consciously taking them in:

- **Your voice:** *How* you say it is as important as *what* you say.
- **Body language:** A subject in its own right and something about which much has been written and said. In essence, your body movements express what your attitudes and thoughts *really* are. You might like to **check out this web page**.
- **Appearance:** First impressions influence the audience's attitudes to you. Dress appropriately for the occasion.

As with most personal skills **oral communication cannot be taught**. Instructors can only point the way. So as always, ***practice is essential***, both to improve your skills generally and also to make the best of each individual presentation you make.

Preparation

Prepare the structure of the talk carefully and logically, just as you would for a written report. What are:

- the objectives of the talk?
- the main points you want to make?

Make a list of these two things as your starting point.

Write out the presentation in rough, just like the first draft of a written report. Review the draft. You will find things that are irrelevant or superfluous - delete them. Check the story is consistent and flows smoothly. If there are things you cannot easily express, possibly because of doubt about your understanding, it is better to leave them unsaid.

Never read from a script. It is also unwise to have the talk written out in detail as a prompt sheet - the chances are you will not locate the thing you want to say amongst all the other text. You should know most of what you want to say - if you don't then you should not be giving the talk! So prepare ***cue cards*** which have key words and phrases (and possibly sketches) on them. Postcards are ideal for this. **Don't forget to number the cards** in case you drop them.

Remember to mark on your cards the visual aids that go with them so that the right OHP or slide is shown at the right time.

Rehearse your presentation - to yourself at first and then in front of some friends. The initial rehearsal should consider how the words and the sequence of visual aids go together. How will you make effective use of your visual aids?

Making the presentation

Greet the audience (*for example*, 'Good morning, everyone and tell them who you are. Then follow this formula for:

- tell the audience what you are going to tell them,
- then tell them,
- at the end tell them what you have told them.

Keep to the time allowed. If you can, keep it short. It's better to under-run than over-run. As a rule of thumb, allow 2 minutes for each *general* overhead transparency or powerpoint slide you use, but longer for any that you want to use for developing specific points. 35 mm slides are generally used more sparingly and stay on the screen longer. However, the audience will get bored with something on the screen for more than 5 minutes, especially if you are not actively talking about it. So switch the display off, or replace the slide with some form of 'wallpaper' such as a company logo.

Stick to the plan for the presentation, don't be tempted to digress - you will eat up time and could end up in a dead-end with no escape!

Unless explicitly told not to, leave time for discussion - 5 minutes is sufficient to allow clarification of points. The session chairman may extend this if the questioning becomes interesting.

At the end of your presentation ask if there are any questions - avoid being terse when you do this as the audience may find it intimidating (*i.e.* it may come across as *any questions? - If there are, it shows you were not paying attention)*. If questions are slow in coming, you can start things off by asking a question of the audience - so have one prepared.

Delivery

Speak clearly. Don't shout or whisper - judge the acoustics of the room.

Don't rush, or talk deliberately slowly. Be natural - although not conversational.

Deliberately pause at key points - this has the effect of emphasising the importance of a particular point you are making.

Avoid jokes - always disastrous unless you are a natural expert.

To make the presentation interesting, change your delivery, but not to obviously, *e.g.*:

- speed
- pitch of voice

Use your hands to emphasise points but don't indulge in to much hand-waving. People can, over time, develop irritating habits. Ask colleagues occasionally what they think of your style.

Look at the audience as much as possible, but don't fix on an individual - it can be intimidating. Pitch your presentation towards the back of the audience, especially in larger rooms.

Don't face the display screen behind you and talk to it. Other annoying habits include:

- Standing in a position where you obscure the screen. In fact, positively check for anyone in the audience who may be disadvantaged and try to accommodate them.
- Muttering over a transparency on the OHP projector plate and not realising that you are blocking the projection of the image. It is preferable to point to the screen than the foil on the OHP (apart from the fact that you will probably dazzle yourself with the brightness of the projector)

Avoid moving about too much. Pacing up and down can unnerve the audience, although some animation is desirable.

Keep an eye on the **audience's** body language. Know when to stop and also when to cut out a piece of the presentation.

Model of the Communication Cycle

- **In our interactive world, every act of communication deeply influences the nature of life in our communities.**

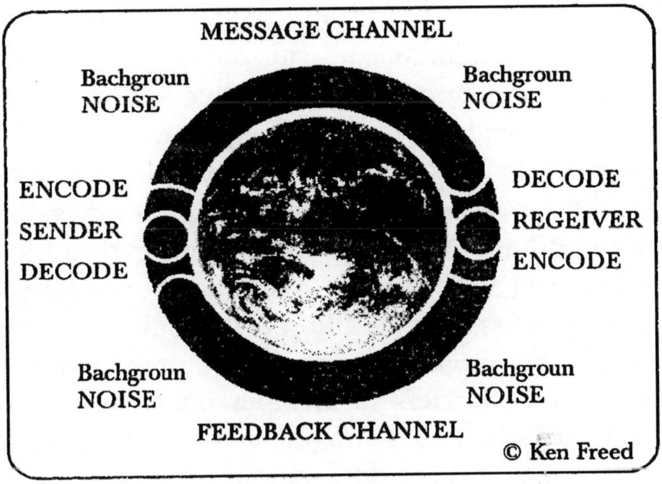

Communication Creates Reality

The communication cycle is fairly easy to understand.

Within any noisy universe, a sender encodes a *verbal* or *nonverbal* message, sends it through any message channel to a receiver, who decodes the message. The receiver then encodes a reply, which is returned through a feedback channel to the sender, who decodes it, deals with it somehow, and perhaps sends another message. Without the full loop communcation is incomplete.

Our individual acts of communication are how each of us makes sense of reality. Our "sense-making" communication habits form all our relations.

The way individuals interact in families is reproduced within the formal and informal organizations in their lives. These groups construct the institutions comprising the communities composing the diverse cultures and societies constituting our nations and our world. As the dominant species on earth, our habitual ways of interacting are imprinted on the planetary systems, reflecting our choices.

Communication spins the web of life. All life is interactive.

How we communicate with ourselves and with others, produces the nature of where we live and breath and have our being. "Senders" and "receivers" interacting (like *yin* and *yang*) generate life itself. Our interactions create our realities,

Conflicts can stem from encoding and decoding errors or assumptions. A filtering system has evolved to help us humans deal with sensory overload. Every outgoing and incoming message gets filtered through the cultural and genetic biases implanted in our minds for pattern recognition. Unconscious barriers to intrapersonal and interpersonal communication tend to fragment our awarenesss. We filter out data incongruent with our mindset. Divisions persist between our perceptions and reality (if "reality" may be known).

We tend to evolve *split perceptions* to hide from ourselves the truths about reality that we wish to avoid. Our split perceptions enable us to believe we live separate and apart from others in our world, that we can get away with any outrage to ourselves or to others. We suffer from the delusion that we may escape the consequences of interactivity. We see what we want to see and hear what we want to hear. We pretend we are not pretending. We are blind by choice. Ignorance is bondage.

Understanding interactivity is the key to healthy communication. We can transform our selves and our world by changing the way we communicate with ourselves and others. Every thought, word and deed sends out ripples altering life for everyone. That's the nature of communication. That's the nature of life in an interactive universe. Why not accept it? A global sense of our deep interactivity inspires responsible self-rule.

❑ ❑ ❑